CHASING

My Dreams

FROM TRAUMATIC BURNS TO TRIUMPHANT SURVIVAL

BARBARA KAMMERER QUAYLE
WITH MONA KRUEGER

STRATTON
—PRESS—
Publishing Life

CHASING MY DREAMS
Copyright © 2021 **Barbara Kammerer Quayle**

Stratton Press Publishing
831 N Tatnall Street Suite M #188,
Wilmington, DE 19801
www.stratton-press.com
1-888-323-7009

ISBN (Paperback): 978-1-64895-442-9
ISBN (Ebook): 978-1-64895-443-6

Printed in the United States of America

DEDICATION

I dedicate this book to every burn survivor and anyone with
a facial or body difference throughout the world who is

Chasing Their Dreams.

I have been honored to know many of you and pray for you
as you work toward a successful and productive life.
I also dedicate this book to Judy and Ken
who are my forever anchors!

CONTENTS

———

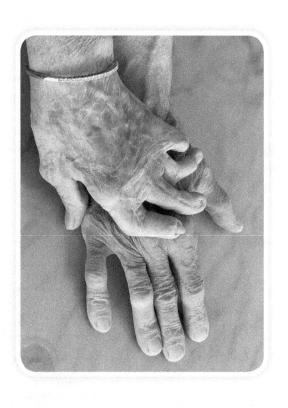

GRATITUDE

I'm grateful to Mona Krueger, who encouraged me to tell my story and joined me as co-author on our ups and downs of the creative journey.

I am so thankful to have been treated in the USA at the University of California Irvine Burn Center, an American Burn Association verified burn center. I was blessed to have such skilled physicians from Dr. Robert Klein and Dr. Robert Bartlett, to Dr. David Furnas, Chief of the Department of Plastic Surgery who gave me back my life. The nursing staff, particularly Clara Rodriguez and Beth Lukina, lessened the pain and fear with their gentle and supportive care.

Great gratitude goes to the Phoenix Society for Burn Survivors, led by friend Amy Acton, who each year raises the bar for aftercare programs for survivors and families, and who provided the cover photo for Chasing My Dreams.

The gratitude never ends for my dear friend, Judy Phillips, who was my anchor through it all and beyond. I'm not sure I could have done it without her.

I am always grateful for my mother, Peggy, and my Aunt Genevieve who prayed for me constantly. Their stalwart support was such a blessing. I am humbled that God heard their prayers.

I am truly forever thankful that God gave me a precious husband like Ken, who has always encouraged and loved me, who quiets my concerns. My next license plate will read TG4KCQ (Thank God for Ken Carl Quayle)

And finally, thank you, Lord, for the remarkable people who I have been honored to call friends and colleagues through the years.

PROLOGUE

———

Each year in the US, 650,000 Americans seek care for some kind of burn injury. Around 75,000 of them get admitted to a burn center for specialized treatment.

The causes vary, from scald injuries to cookstove grease fires, adding accelerants to backyard bonfires, car accidents, house fires, and suicide attempts, to name a few.

A severe burn injury is a life-altering injury. The physical and emotional recovery takes years. Everyone surrounding the burn survivor is affected as well.

This book is the story of my personal journey as a burn survivor, but in many ways, it is the story of all the beautiful souls who have become stronger, more compassionate, and whose stories are often compelling. We wear our scars with humility and strength. We want to be good citizens, fit in, and live life to the fullest. Our hope is that you will gain new insights and compassion for a group of brave folks.

1

Rocketing

My girlfriend's surprise birthday party was in full swing when my boyfriend Murray and I drove into the upscale subdivision of Huntington Beach, California. The beautifully landscaped ranch-style home belonged to one of his clients.

Navigating the clay-tiled pathway to the front door, I breathed in the February Orange County air, a mix of crisp ocean breezes, and the delicate smell of wood burning in a neighbor's fireplace. I lived for weekend gatherings with friends, a chance to meet new people and engage in stimulating conversations. Our hostess with golden-tanned arms, dressed in a sleeveless blue pantsuit, greeted us with enthusiasm. She ushered us into a kitchen abuzz with chatter from milling guests clustered around a buffet table. The house had a midcentury modern aesthetic. Rich woods and fabrics in neutrals and pastels conveyed a welcome feel.

We headed to the large granite island where my favorite Grgich Hills Estate chardonnay from Napa sat cooling in a silver bucket. We both accepted a glass from the guest of honor and looked around for familiar faces. I recognized a gentleman from a previous get-together, and we walked over his way to say hi.

"Barbara, Murray, so nice to see you again. How are you two doing?" asked Ben, a plastic surgeon who had used Murray's CPA firm for years.

"We're good," said Murray, "though Barbara keeps dragging me from place to place, the social creature that she is."

"Yeah right," I said. "Don't let him fool you. He loves a good party as much as I do."

"True, but unlike you, I'm not the last guest hanging on into the wee hours. It's that all-girls Catholic college you went to—made you hungry for male company," Murray said.

"Really?" asked Ben.

"You are forgetting about the all-*boys* Catholic college right down the road. I never want for male attention," I retorted.

We all shared a chuckle and talked about our travel plans to go to Wimbledon for the summer matches.

We eventually wandered off. Murray and I slowly made the rounds, introducing ourselves to new people as we went. After a long week of teaching English and journalism to junior high students, adult conversation lured me like a sale on high-end shoes. I was energized by the connections and the laughter.

At some point in the evening, Murray and I became separated between the kitchen and the family room, pulled into different conversations.

At a lull between chats, I glanced around to find him. I glimpsed his dark brown curls through the arch into the dining room. He stood by the paneled archway into the living room, lean and strong. With brown eyes and a year-round California tan, he appealed to me on many levels. We met on a blind date arranged by my good friends, Judy and Bobby, a few years ago. We shared a deep love of tennis and spent every weekend together. I thought we made a great couple. We both were happy in our individual careers, liked similar sports and outings, our mutual friends melded, and we always had something to talk about. The relationship was neither clingy nor conflicted. We could share about sensitive topics, agree or disagree, and had respect for our mutual need for time apart.

By 11:00 p.m., the party seemed to be winding down, and Murray caught my eye from across the room, mouthing his readiness to leave. When I pretended to ignore him, he walked over and interrupted my conversation with another partygoer.

"Barbara, I'll go get the car. Meet you out front in five minutes."

I watched him leave and rolled my eyes. "Sorry for that... What were you saying?" I asked. Not quite ready to give up the conversation, I continued chatting.

Murray popped his head back into the house with an exasperated look on his face minutes later, gesturing for me to speed it up. My new acquaintance graciously finished up her story. We said goodbye to our hosts and took our leave, promising to have another get-together soon.

* * *

The silver Nissan 260z sports car buzzed through the quiet neighborhood into busy Warner Avenue traffic on our way to Murray's home. He was in love with his car. I think he felt like it bolstered his newly single-guy image after a recent divorce. Warner bustled with activity, the clubs and restaurants hosting revelers out for a good time on a Saturday night.

The couple glasses of chardonnay and the smooth ride of the car lulled me into sleepy euphoria. The black wool slacks, white silk blouse, and loosely woven sweater I had donned earlier helped to ward off the late-night chill. The smell of leather seats mixed with Murray's favorite cologne added to my calm.

"You looked great tonight," Murray said, his deep brown eyes straying from the asphalt to briefly catch mine. His curls caught the beam of a streetlight flashing into the space between us.

I had my mother's thick dark hair worn in a Dorothy Hamill bob, all the rage in 1977. My curtain of hair swung gently as I answered and turned back to look out the window. "I'm glad you think so," I said, accepting the compliment at face value while tamping down the do-you-really-know-who-I-am question that had lingered in my thoughts as of late.

I wondered where the relationship was heading. Better to change the subject. The February night's post-party vibe felt too mellow to focus on disturbing questions.

"Did you know Ben's latest love is a junior high English teacher like I am? We shared war stories and some combat techniques," I said.

Back in my college years, a professor had tried to steer me away from a secondary education credential, believing my small stature of 5'2" would be a deterrent to handling a bunch of know-it-all teens. Sadly, I believed him for way too long. I almost gave up the idea of being a teacher entirely, taking off a year of school and working. But I couldn't find a career that appealed to me more than teaching. And after some time had passed, I mustered a little gumption, defied my professor's words, and never looked back. Teaching junior high simply required a saying-what-you-mean-and-meaning-what-you-say attitude, coupled with a backbone. I taught by a motto learned from a master teacher at the beginning of my career: "Be firm, friendly, and fair."

Having lost my father at the age of twelve, I felt their angst more than most. A thinly veiled neediness. A hunger to fit in. The student body at my junior high school had labeled me the strict-but-smiling grammar despot. I assigned them tortuous tasks, like writing perfect paragraphs at the beginning of class on a daily basis. Mastering the English language played a key role in their education. How successfully they would wield this tool could make or break their future careers. They heard it every class.

"We agreed we both love the energy and the skills the kids gain in a year's time," I said to Murray.

"You ladies can have that job," he said, bringing my thoughts back to our conversation. "I'll take my quiet CPA office and adult clientele any day."

Being a CPA with his own small business gave him flexibility and enough money to contribute to the support of his two young

14

daughters from his former marriage. They were sweet and fun girls whom I loved to hang out with on the weekends Murray had them.

With a failed marriage of my own behind me, I was looking for someone very special who could be trusted for the long haul. Murray was a good man and could prove to be the one I was looking for. *Give him a chance*, I told myself. *It's too early to know.*

That night, the sports car felt cozy and safe, the city lights romantic. The endless line of cars streaming along didn't annoy. Waiting at a traffic light to access the freeway, I declared my existence good. Peaceful. Maybe even bordering somewhere near happy.

* * *

"Barbara? Barbara. It's okay. It's going to be okay."

The voice sounded far off, tunneled. I recognized pain, confusion, my senses blurred. A beeping sound bounced around the bed I was lying on. My mouth felt stone dry, and strange smells assaulted my nostrils. Disinfectant? Something rotting? The fog lifted long enough to grasp the word *hospital.*

Awakening to caricatures in lab coats with concerned expressions bending over me, I wasn't sure what was real. I felt like an actor in a bad soap opera.

"What am I doing in a hospital?" I asked. I became aware of bandages, a tight weaving of them on my body, face, and hands.

"You were burned," a voice said quietly.

My thoughts jumped, frantically. I quickly tried to chronicle the past evening and had not even a vague recollection of anything that could have severely burned me. In this era of the threat of nuclear bombs from Russia, only one possibility loomed in my mind.

"Was there a nuclear attack?"

My question so puzzled the staff, they wondered if I had suffered a head injury and followed the protocol, asking the basics every few minutes:

"What is your name?"

"Where do you live?"

"When were you born?"

And all the while I tried to process other pieces of information being thrown around the room.

Thirty-five percent.

Second and third degree.

Facial burns.

Fingers badly damaged.

"Murray. Where is Murray?" I asked.

He came into focus at my bedside with bandages wrapped around his hands and neck. My confusion increased as I realized he was up walking around, while I was in a hospital bed hardly able to move. And then a glimmer of memory from the previous day surfaced.

"What happened?" I whispered. "How badly am I burned?"

His silence scared me. Why did he keep staring at me and then looking away? I wanted to shout at him, demand him to focus and answer my questions. He finally managed to say, "It was a Buick... an old Buick rear-ended us at the stoplight, and the Nissan exploded. I was knocked out. I guess a cop passing by saw the crash and called it in. They pulled me out, but they didn't know about you...and I wasn't coherent to tell them, to help you...I'm sorry...so sorry, babe."

I fought to remember. "What happened with the Buick?"

"Nothing. I guess the guys panicked and ran. The cops said they were illegal immigrants and fearful of getting caught. A bystander heard you whimper and thought it was a hurt dog inside. He reached across the console and dragged you out the driver's side door. The paramedics brought us both to the burn center at the University of California Irvine. We were only thirty minutes from here."

"How bad are my burns?"

"Your face is swollen. They say your cheeks and chin are the deepest. Your right hand too. And your back. We won't know anything for a while. We have to wait and see how things heal." I processed his words, a million more questions rising to the surface. I didn't feel a lot of pain. Was that good or bad? Weren't burns supposed to be really painful? When could I go home? Would it take a week? Who would take my classes at school?

"Stop worrying. I can see your panic," Murray said. "I love you...We'll get through this." He squeezed my arm gently. "And I'll never let anything bad happen to you ever again."

I clung to his words. I desperately wanted them to be true. Maybe they meant that he really did love me, that we had a real future together.

I told myself the burns couldn't be as bad as they said and forced the panic down. Exhausted by the morning's events and the medications flowing through my body, I fell into a deep sleep.

I woke again hours later to whispered voices near my bed. I tried to shrug off the sleepiness to take in my surroundings. A familiar cologne clued me in to the identity of my visitors.

"Bobby? Judy?" I asked.

"Yes, Barbara, we're here."

I tried to open my eyes to see them, but my vision was hazy at best. I felt a warm hand hold lightly to my arm.

"We just want to sit with you for a while," said Judy. "Let us know if you need anything."

"Why can't I see?" I asked.

"The doctor said the burns have caused your eyelids to swell shut, but they are monitoring everything very closely. It will subside in a few days."

"Why don't I feel a lot of pain? Don't burns really hurt?"

"You are being given a lot of medication, Barbara," Bob said. "Your nurse was just in here with a dose." His deep voice reassured me.

I was thankful for both of them. We had been friends for years. Judy and I had met at United California Bank in downtown Long Beach, where we both worked when I first moved to the West Coast in 1964. I worked in the loan department, and Judy was secretary to the president. We became good friends. Both being single at the time, we often double-dated. Judy epitomized all the characteristics of an extraordinary friend—loyal, sensitive, caring. Bob had a teddy bear personality, with an infectious laugh guaranteed to make a person smile. Murray and I had spent a lot of time with them. We played tennis together, often dining out and taking in the Orange County culture.

"Did Murray leave?" I asked.

"I think he went back to his room," Judy said. "He'll visit again soon."

I felt my attention wavering, struggling to take in her words. "Love you guys," I managed to whisper as I drifted off into the outer atmosphere of drug wonderland.

* * *

It was day 6 of my hospital stay when I awoke to throbbing pain across the entire surface of my back. It felt like my condition was getting worse, not better. It seemed I had been lying here so much longer than a week. I vacillated between numbing my emotions to cope and crying at will. A daily routine had been established, and I learned to grit my teeth and endure it. Murray had been discharged the day before, but planned to return in a week for a surgery to patch the back of his neck with a small graft. He promised to visit whenever he had the chance.

I heard footsteps entering my cubicle and braced myself for the beginning of a new round of care.

"Barbara, my name is Clara, and I'll be your nurse today. I'm going to take very good care of you. How was your night? Are you in a lot of pain this morning?"

"I woke up a lot. My back is hurting something fierce," I said.

"You are due for a new round of pain medication. I will put it into your IV straight away," she replied.

With my eyes still swollen shut, I couldn't see the woman with the soft, reassuring voice. It took a few more weeks to see her elegant face and figure, tender brown eyes, and kind smile. But it took only minutes for my senses to absorb her gentleness. She was an anchor in this new and frightening place. I would cling to the gift of her secure and safe presence through multiple procedures and learn to trust her implicitly.

My bandages had to be changed twice a day, once in the tub room in the morning and a second time at my bedside in the evening. I dreaded both. An IV dripped steadily via a line in my forearm, antibiotic fluids keeping my body from sepsis and dehydration. My bandaged hands rested on pillows on each side of me.

Clara administered the promised pain medication and told me she would be right back to take me to the tub room.

Clara wheeled me down the hallway to the hydro tub room, which I came to label the torture chamber. The hydro tub was a necessary evil where the dead and damaged skin had to be removed to prepare the area for a skin graft or to facilitate the growth of new skin cells on a less severely burned area. The hydro room had a platform with a hydraulic lift that would swing me over and into the water. The wound care nurse stood outside on a platform to reach me. The Silvadene was washed off and a session of debridement done. Fortunately for me, Clara would administer a dose of ketamine before she began the painful procedure.

"Now, Barbara, think of a place you would like to be and something you enjoy. We want you to be in a good frame of mind."

I often imagined hosting a dinner party and planning the table settings. Or I would be in Hawaii on the beach relaxing with a book. These thoughts kept me from a side effect of the drug, horrendous hallucinations. I would wake up in bed an hour later in excruciating pain, but relieved to have the procedure behind me.

When the evening shift of nurses arrived, the tone of the day changed from a torrent of constant activity and treatments to a mellow pace. Clara's replacement for the night was a young athletic nurse named Beth, fresh out of nursing school and exuding more energy than one of my junior high kids, if that were possible. Though the day was winding down, I still had another round of bandage changes to endure.

"Hi, Barbara. I'm Beth, and I have the privilege of being your nurse tonight. How are you feeling?" she asked as more pain meds plunged into my bloodstream from the syringe she administered, preparing me for the procedure to come.

"Kind of a rough day, but I'm hanging in there," I said, trying not to dread the evening ritual. "Distract me, please. Tell me about your life. I remember something about a guy named Warren? What have you two been up to?"

Beth's current boyfriend shared her passion for hiking and bicycling, and the regaling of their adventures together kept the dread at bay. Beth's distinctive Bostonian accent entertained me while her air of competence fostered trust. I liked her laugh and sense of humor. Plus, I knew she cared.

"Barbara, before I tell you how I almost flipped over a mountain cliff last weekend, there is just one small thing I need to do. Don't be alarmed, but your NG tube has dislodged and needs to be reinserted."

Her words started my heart pounding. I hated the feeding tube and the feeling of it in my throat, especially *moving* in my throat.

"Okay. I trust you know what you're doing?"

"Of course, Barbara, piece of cake…Just give me a few moments."

My body clenched tight as I felt the tube moving slowly along my nasal passage farther and farther down. I tried not to gag.

"There, that does it," she said with obvious relief.

The sigh made me suspicious.

"Beth, you have done that before, right?"

"Well… not exactly. It was the first time. But I knew what I was doing."

We both burst into laughter.

I wanted to scold her, but I sighed instead, shaking my head. "Fool me once, but next time, I won't be so trusting!"

But thankfully I could be. Even as a young nurse right out of college, Beth worked competently like a seasoned professional. I braced myself for the evening bandage change. One more round of care, and I could have some peace for the night.

Beth tilted me on my side to allow access to the burned area on my back. I felt like a dazed and drugged mummy, until gentle hands began to peel off the sticky, bloodstained gauze. As the bandages pulled free, the air alone created intense pain on the open flesh. I found out the reason I hadn't felt a lot of pain the first few days was because the burns were so deep, the nerves numbed and damaged by the injury, to be awakened slowly but surely during the treatment process. Each tug caused me to jolt in response. Gasping, I tried hard to control the flinches.

"Barbara, try to relax. I know this is painful. I will be as careful as I can. Let me know when you need a break."

The lack of control, anticipating the pain, kept me on edge. Beth's competent tone, succinct step-by-step explanation, and offered choices conveyed her sincere empathy. I reached for trust.

The pain sharpened as the layers pulled free.

"I need a break," I rasped out, waiting for some of the sharp pain to subside, fighting not to sob.

"Okay. Catch your breath. One step done. I just have to clean up the edges a bit and reapply the Silvadene and bandages."

The cleanup part felt like sandpaper scraping on raw nerves. Even a soft sponge touching any of the exposed flesh was excruciating. My body clenched and tried to endure. My stomach started to roil, despite the antacid and morphine given to me before the procedure began.

As she worked, Beth tried to soothe me. "I know it feels like torture, but we change the bandages twice a day for a purpose, to help remove the damaged skin and lessen the chance of infection. One more small area, and we will be finished for today, Barbara. You are doing great. Try to keep still a little longer…"

Thrashing to get away from the pain, hearing Beth's reassuring voice stilled my jerky movements.

Just a little longer.

Clara and Beth.

With a life rocketed out of control, the longer I was under their care, the more I realized they were two irreplaceable gifts tethering me to stable ground.

2

Decisions

An authoritative male voice coming from the side of my hospital bed jarred me awake. "Barbara, it's Dr. Klein."

My pulse always jumped when a doctor spoke to me. It was day number 10 of my hospital stay. A feeling of "what next?" always hovered. The little unknowns in every encounter with staff members stalked my emotional well-being. There seemed to be this constant need for painful procedures: repositioning me, tweaking a splint, swapping a catheter or IV line, changing bandages, and stretching with physical and occupational therapy. I feared every new person entering my cubicle to transport me somewhere, wondering if they would be gentle. I was vigilant about sounds and movement around the unit, dreading the next event I had no control over. It was old hat for the staff, having taken care of hundreds of patients, but a very unfamiliar and frightening reality for me.

Dr. Klein was a burn surgeon in his thirties, with premature gray hair and kind blue eyes. Hailing from Ohio, he had a Midwest directness about him that gave me confidence in his abilities. This day, his calm tone flowed out of the surgical mask he wore over his nose and mouth, part of the protective garments anyone entering my cubicle had to don.

"We need to discuss your first surgical procedure. I would like to take some skin from your left thigh and graft it onto your forehead and upper cheeks, where the burns are the deepest."

His words raised scary questions. Lying in this hospital room for the past ten days had been a blur of scattered information and uncertainty about my future.

"Will it leave scars?"

His eyes never left mine. "Not having surgery will leave more scars," he firmly replied.

"More scars implies some scars."

He blinked, and his right hand moved up to adjust his mask, pausing as if searching for words. "Barbara, I know you're frightened. I wish I could tell you that your face will heal perfectly, but we have to wait and see. The area around your jawline and mouth we will let heal on their own and hope for minimal scarring. They aren't burned as deeply. But we need to work on the areas that are deep. Let's take this one surgery at a time."

"Minimal…"

Could I live with minimal? What did minimal look like?

I clung to the thought that plastic surgery could restore my appearance. I had my role to play: comply with staff demands, endure waking up from the daily debridement sessions in great pain, and adhere to the evening routine of bandage changes.

Part of me balked at being in the passenger seat of my own life. But for the time being, any control I thought I had was an illusion.

* * *

"How bad does my face look?"

It was the question I had been dying to ask but scared to pose. Propped up in my hospital bed two weeks later, I finally ventured into the taboo subject with my friend Judy. She had been a steady and encouraging presence at my bedside. I trusted her like no other. Judy was petite like me. I noticed her azure blue eyes and soft wavy hair that curled delicately around her face in a whole new way, even while I feared for my own appearance. I looked at her hands, long angular fingers, manicured nails. Would my fingers be okay? Functional? Scarred?

The cubicle boasted handmade cards from my students and coworkers, which hung neatly with a string across the curtain that separated my bed from the next one over. A "Get Well" Minnie Mouse balloon drooped slightly in the far corner. A stuffed teddy bear with a heart-shaped ribbon perched on a small chair below the balloon, a token of love from Murray.

I expected an honest answer to the question about my face. Judy tempered truth.

"The parts I can see are kind of red and blotchy, though some of the swelling has gone down. They said it will improve with time," she said, "and you already know a notch on the outside edge of each nostril is missing."

"No! I didn't realize. What do you mean by notch…How big is a notch?" I asked. "Nobody told me that."

I continued before she had a chance to speak, not really wanting to know the answer.

"Wait. No. Dr. Klein said this is temporary. They have to let the tissue do whatever it wants for the first few months after grafting, and then they can go back and fix it."

After a round of debridement in the tub earlier that morning, I caught a glimpse of myself in a metal panel on the way back to my cubicle. That distant glance brought on a level of panic I didn't know what to do with. Underneath my seeming openness to discuss my injury, I really couldn't handle knowing the full extent. I pledged to avoid any reflective or shiny surface for a while. I closed or averted my eyes during bandage changes. It was all just too frightening.

"Temporary," Judy said, her brow descending, her teeth biting her lower lip. "We have to be patient."

Judy was one of a handful of friends taking shifts to be with me. Murray visited when he could, but it was tax season, and his job made great demands on his time. I was somewhat alone in the world except for my friends. An only child, I had lost my father to a heart attack when I was twelve years old. I was my mother's whole world. Though outwardly she appeared strong, she masked her emotions by holding everything inside. I understood the toll my injuries would take and wanted to protect her. Besides an aunt, my mother was the only surviving member of our relatives who we were close to. She had buried her husband, her parents, and all her siblings. Hardly able to sustain myself emotionally from day to day, I feared having her at the hospital would be too much for both of us. To see me in so much pain would be devastating for her. I feared she would fall apart, and I knew I was not in any state to give her support. I could hardly get through a day of holding myself up.

Judy suggested that I arrange for the staff to connect us through a telephone call. We had to carefully choose a time when I wasn't in a morphine stupor and would be able to speak sensibly. While on morphine, sometimes I would have a thought to convey and, in midsentence, lose my ability to complete it. It was frustrating and exhausting. This call had to be a team effort.

We finally arranged a 4:00 p.m. call after my daily tub room procedure and dressing change. The morphine would be at a lower level and my thought process more coherent. Judy held the phone to my ear since I had no use of my injured hands. Mother had been informed that we would be calling at an exact time and picked up on the first ring.

"Hello, Barbara," came her anxious voice over the line.

"Mother, I am so happy to hear your voice. I know you must be worried, but I am doing fine," I said, trying to hold back my tears.

"You sound weak," she said hesitantly.

"I have to go through a lot of care every day, and at the end, I am tired is all."

"I'd like to come there to see you and help you, honey."

"Mother, I think it is best if you wait until I get home because I am not awake much now, and I am so tired. I'll feel better when I am discharged." I didn't want to tell her how my burns looked or see the sadness in her eyes at realizing how fire had changed her daughter forever.

"Okay, honey, whatever you think best," she replied.

In my effort to have a normal conversation, I said, "Mother, have you been up to visit Aunt Gen?" Aunt Gen was the one called about the accident, and she drove the thirty miles to her sister-in-law's home in Iowa to break the news in person.

"Yes, I drove up to have lunch with her last week, and we talked about you the whole time. She told me the nuns at the convent were all praying for you."

"Oh, that's so comforting. Please thank them for me," I said. "Mother, I'm going to have to hang up because I'm fading."

"I understand, honey, and please call me more often so I will know how things are going. Remember I love you, Barbara."

"I love you too, Mommy," I choked out.

Judy hung up the phone, and I let the tears flow. I wished my dad were alive so he could be there to comfort her.

"Your aunt has been checking in with me every day and giving the updates to your mom," said Judy. "We can keep doing that if you don't have the energy for more phone calls."

Making plans and organizing tasks kept me from dwelling too deeply on my injuries and all the unknowns. My coping skills appeared to be working. I tried to be upbeat when people visited me; my social skills took over. A burn center was a scary place to visit. Why make it tough on anyone who was nice enough to come and see me? I didn't question the incongruity of that. My friends were one of my lifelines, and driving them away was the last thing I wanted to do. So they took their cues from me.

* * *

The next morning, Dr. Klein walked into my room, his steps brisk and purposeful. I was in the middle of eating breakfast, congealed eggs dripping from the fork, my stiff and bandaged left hand awkwardly holding the modified utensil, a puffy Styrofoam piece fitted around the handle. The right hand I couldn't use at all.

"Barbara, we have to talk about your right hand."

Dr. Klein's image sharpened as I focused on his face. With the swelling of my eyelids reduced, I could see his serious expression, the slight fidgeting of his hands.

I looked at him warily, dropping the fork onto the tray. "Okay…"

I had glimpsed my brownish fingers through the water of the Hubbard tub without bandages and had been purposefully avoiding a reality I feared.

Dr. Klein tried to lay it out gently. His kind eyes narrowed slightly, focusing intently on my face as he stood near the bed. "We can leave your fingers a while longer, but there is a risk of infection. If that happens, you could lose more tissue at the base of your fingers."

I struggled to take in his words.

"Our other option is to amputate them now to prevent that from happening. The decision is yours."

"Fingers…meaning all my fingers? You have to take all of them?"

He looked away, sighed, and returned his gaze to my face. "I'm sorry, Barbara, but that is the safest option. There isn't enough viable tissue left to even attempt to graft your fingers…I'll give you some time to think about it. How about I check back in after rounds?"

I nodded my head numbly and watched him leave, my eyes unfocused, my mind reeling. Of the ten initial surgeries I had to undergo, this one was the most horrifying.

Four fingers and a thumb.

My dominant hand. My writing hand. My tennis racket–holding hand.

An inconceivable loss.

I tried to picture myself using my left hand to swing the tennis racket, Murray and I back on track after my recovery. I would once again be in my cute tennis outfits showing off my tan, zipping across the court with the new skills of a leftie. It was conceivable that I could learn to use my opposite hand. My love of tennis ran deep. I had always thought of myself as playing the game into my eighties, the perfect retirement recreation and means of staving off old age. And extra pounds.

I certainly didn't want to risk more tissue loss on the right hand. Every millimeter was precious.

What didn't enter my mind was the possibility that the fingers of my left hand wouldn't be as straight and perfect as I envisioned, nor the skin on my beautiful legs after donor sites took their toll. Those realities would be revealed at a later time.

On this day, the decision had to be based on what I knew in the moment.

I felt the loneliest I had ever felt in my thirty-three years of existence. I longed for someone to help me make this life-altering decision, someone strong who would tell me all would be okay, fingers or no fingers. The silence in the cubicle reminded me I was on my own. Tax season had overtaken Murray, and the rarity of his appearances worried me when I was feeling down and insecure. Lately an everyday occurrence.

Dr. Klein returned much too soon. How could I get the words out? How could I tell him to basically cut off my hand?

But what choice did I really have?

"Go ahead and amputate," I told him, my voice shaky. "I trust your judgment."

Our eyes collided and held.

He gently touched my shoulder to reassure me. "All right, Barbara. I will set up the surgery. I wish we had a better option, but we just don't."

He didn't linger in the room.

All alone once again, I felt a lead weight on my chest pressing me into the bed. I tried to breathe past the suffocating feelings. The decision had been made. There was no going back.

* * *

The unveiling occurred slowly, layers of gauze winding off for the reveal. Six days post-surgery, I dreaded the first look at my right hand. Or what I imagined was left of it. My forearm rested on the table next to the bed. I tried not to flinch at the tug of the blood-soaked bandages. As the last layer pulled free, I saw a little ball with stitched-up tissue over knuckle bones. Morbidly wondering what they did with my precious fingers, all I could picture was them lying in some red-labeled bio waste bin.

Breathe. Just keep breathing.

Dr. Klein voiced his satisfaction with how well the site looked, without any sign of infection; the area was still swollen but healing well.

"We saved a good amount of the base tissue, Barbara. We will be able to cut through the area between the thumb and index finger joint to give you a pincher-like movement in a future surgery. You should be able to write and grip things. It will help immensely with everyday tasks."

Looking up, he grimaced at the sight of my tears. He tried to comfort me with words of empathy.

"I know it's hard. But you made the right decision."

Shirley, my occupational therapist, arrived at my bedside as Dr. Klein made his exit. She had gorgeous auburn hair, cut short and curled at the nape of her neck that I always envied. Her British accent and tall, lean frame lent a commanding, no-nonsense air to our interactions. My name, uttered from her lips, sounded like "Bob" instead of "Barb." It was one of the most endearing traits about her.

She came in waving a piece of white plastic and talking a mile a minute. Her piercing blue eyes were lit up with excitement. Being totally focused on her patients' recovery was how she operated, but this contraption had me wondering what was in store for me.

"I did it, Bob! I think it's my best creation ever," she boasted, lifting up her prize, wearing a satisfied smile.

The thing looked otherworldly to me. It was a stiff white mask, designed to be contoured to the natural lines of my face. The opaque, thick plastic material called Orthoplast would provide necessary pressure on my new facial grafts to keep them flat and smooth. Scar tissue needs time to mature and can grow indiscriminately and profusely if not constrained.

"So this is the thing I have to wear twenty-three hours a day for the next how many months?" I asked, swallowing hard and fighting back more tears.

This day just kept getting better.

Noticing my response, Shirley's smile dimmed.

"For the foreseeable future, yes…I know it doesn't feel like it right now, but this mask is your best friend to keep the scars at a minimum."

Shirley had talked endlessly about the benefits of the white Lone Ranger mask. The new grafts on my face and body would tighten for up to a year as they were maturing. With pressure and a daily therapy routine, I hoped to be able to battle any building scar tissue wanting to contract and pull the tissue too tight. As much as I longed to be a rule breaker at times, my days from Catholic school taught me to follow directions and conform to what's best for me. If this hideous contraption was standing between me and raised thick scars on my face, then, heaven help me, there was no way I would rebel against using it. I resigned myself to hi-ho-silver-away. I wanted to look like I used to.

Shirley carefully fit the mask over my eyes and upper cheeks, attaching a series of Velcro straps across the clumps of hair left on my head.

A cold feeling crept into my chest cavity. The mask felt confining, uncomfortable, and foreign. I didn't even want to think about what I looked like wearing it.

Temporary? Be patient?

The Minnie Mouse balloon drooped another notch in the corner.

* * *

Tax season had finally ended, and I was looking forward to seeing more of Murray. He showed up on a Sunday night in April, day 39 of my time in the burn unit. The first thing I noticed was the outfit: white shorts, blue polo shirt, and tennis shoes. He looked healthy and vibrant, his nose slightly red from a day in the sun playing our favorite sport without me. I tried not to let the distress show in my eyes. It wasn't his fault that he was living his old life while

I was stuck in this place, in this limbo land, not knowing what the future would bring.

"Hi, honey, sorry it's been a couple of weeks, and we've only had phone calls. I'll try to make it up to you now that I don't have to work as much," he said, drawing close to my bed. "Anything new? When can we get you out of here?"

"I think another month or so. At least that's what Dr. Klein is telling me."

"More surgeries?"

"At least two more—one on my back and more on my hands. Some areas might heal on their own, so they are waiting to see if a graft is really necessary. I have started occupational therapy. I have to be able to feed myself and do basic things before they will discharge me."

"How are you holding up?"

I saw the genuine concern in his eyes, the need to try and make things better for me.

"Hanging in there. I can't wait for everything to just be healed. It feels like it's taking forever. The pain doesn't seem to be lessening. And I'm so weak. I can barely move my left hand. Even a plastic fork feels heavy, like it's made of lead."

"I'm working on finding a home care nurse for you when you're ready, and I have a lead on a really excellent plastic surgeon, a Dr. David Furnas. One of my clients told me he wouldn't let anyone else near his wife or daughter with this kind of an injury."

"That sounds promising, but I feel overwhelmed at how much there is yet for me to face—but I am thankful, Murray."

"I told you, babe, we'll get through this together."

I held his words close to my heart and pondered them long after he headed home for the night. Though his visits had been sporadic, I knew he cared about me.

We'll get through this together.

* * *

It was midnight on day 50 of my stay, and the ward had too many distractions for me to sleep. My right wrist sported a long thin metal pin through the center of the residual limb. The pin was attached to pulleys on both sides to hold my arm straight out and fixed. The new postage stamp–sized grafts were exposed to the air and held firmly to the wrist for protection in order for the new skin to heal properly. I wondered what would happen in an emergency, as I couldn't release my arm from the contraption alone. I avoided looking to the right for any length of time. It was too painful to focus on the little stub and all I had lost.

My cubicle was one of eight in a U-shaped configuration, with the nurses' station centered in the middle. The curtains that separated each bed offered minimal protection against noise, smells, and commotion most hours of the day.

An elderly lady had come in three days ago with scald burns, and I listened to her cries for far too many hours. I hadn't heard anything from her bed for the last hour and was relieved she was finally getting a break from her pain.

What had my attention now was the bed to my left. A plane crash in the Canary Islands had caused hundreds of deaths, and our burn ward had absorbed several injured passengers. It was a humanitarian endeavor, but meant less time and attention for each patient as the staff was maxed and stressed to the limit. The halting and labored breathing of the lady next to me had me on edge. I kept waiting for her to either catch her breath or stop breathing entirely.

After a series of disturbing breaths, I pushed my call light for a nurse. It took several long minutes for anyone to respond. Beth finally popped her head in.

"Beth, please check on Mrs. White. Her breaths sound sporadic and are getting worse by the second. I can't sleep. I'm afraid she will stop breathing altogether."

"Okay, I will. Try not to worry. What can I get you to help you sleep?"

"I don't think anything will help. I'm glad our scald burn lady is finally resting quietly. That helps."

"Yes…well. Barbara, I don't want to upset you, but you will find out soon enough that she passed away earlier tonight."

"You mean she died?"

"Her burns were deep…Her body couldn't cope. She was elderly and had a big burn. It happens…"

She touched my foot in sympathy, looking grim. The curtain rustled as she stepped over to check on Mrs. White.

People die from burn injuries.

Why the thought had only just occurred to me didn't register. But I was astounded. And a little panicked. One thought after another raced through my mind. Could I have died? Age and health play a role for sure, but infection can decimate even a healthy person with large portions of skin no longer intact. Surgeries can fail. Pneumonia is a constant threat, even for patients who lived through several surgeries.

The ward took on a new chill. Sleep eluded me for more hours.

Soon, the early morning light filtered into my cubicle. My thoughts concluded.

I could have died. But I didn't.

I looked to the right and stared at my outstretched arm. Life had come at a high price. But I was one of the survivors.

3

Tumbling

"So, word on the floor is that you are getting out of here soon," Clara said, smiling gently as she tugged up the tight zipper of the customized pressure garment I had to wear. They looked like tan leggings that encased me from feet to torso, with a zipper on each side. The zippers allowed the material to be tightened over the contours of my body. I wore a separate vest for the grafts on my arms and back. Gloves were also measured to fit my little right hand and my left.

Clara had just started her twelve-hour shift, and the April sunshine was beaming into my space, promising a warm day.

"I know what you're doing...trying to distract me from thinking about these awful things."

I shifted uncomfortably, trying to mold myself into the tight fabric. If it felt hot and claustrophobic on a spring day, what would a scorching California summer be like?

Wearing these thick garments went against every fashion protocol in existence. But between newly healed grafts and donor sites on a good portion of my body, I reminded myself the pressure was necessary to keep the scars flat and soft as they matured over the next year.

"It is day number 72," I said, "and Dr. Klein promised I could leave by the end of the week."

"To Murray's?"

"Yes. It's been kind of assumed all along, and Murray found a great home health nurse for me who, thank God, my insurance is paying for." Lifting up both hands to make my point, I said, "These wretched, useless hands aren't going to get me far at the moment."

"No, not at the moment," Clara agreed, pausing to catch my attention, "but I see you going far, Barbara...very far."

I appreciated her encouraging words. But the future looked oh so gray and thoughts of what was next overwhelming. I longed for the time when I would be able to live independently again. It seemed a lofty goal. I had much to figure out, but the decision to not give up was the only one that truly mattered today.

* * *

"Do not pass go. Do not collect $200. Get out of here as fast as you can!" Clara whispered with a smile as she accompanied me to the front desk of the burn center, a couple feet from freedom. A few of the staff gathered around, witnesses to my big day, and called out their goodbyes.

"Good luck, Barbara."

"You're gonna do great."

"Be good, but not too good."

Melanie, my new day nurse, followed right behind us. She was a fifty-something take-charge type, a highly experienced burn nurse from the LA area whom Murray found. She brought a high level of burn care knowledge and professionalism that could bridge the gap between the hospital and rehab for me. Melanie understood my need for daily range of motion, good nutrition, and faithful adherence to an aftercare regimen. She knew that it would take months to build back my endurance levels. Her arms clutched several heavy bags, the paraphernalia accumulated during a long hospital stay.

I was elated.

I was terrified.

I stared at the committed souls who prodded, cajoled, and stiff-armed me into getting to this day. They all sported encouraging smiles as they watched me leave the burn center.

"Thanks, everyone. Thanks for all you've done. I hope I can do this without you..."

The door opened before us, and we shuffled out, Clara pushing my wheelchair. The door closed slowly, the burr of the automated hinge ringing a last familiar tune. Clad in my pressure garments and white mask, I took a deep breath as we moved forward.

I *can* do this.

Down this corridor beckoned the sunshine, the missed spring smells, a whole world I had felt cut off from. Too often with jealous pangs I watched my visitors come and go, leading normal lives in normal bodies, untethered to stiff skin and weakness. Despite the physical challenges, today was a triumph.

Melanie hurried ahead to bring the car around, leaving Clara and me by the curved hospital driveway with the bags at our feet. I noticed a few curious glances, but distracted myself by breathing in the warm air, relishing the sounds of traffic and the bustle. The palm trees swayed gently in the breeze, a sight so familiar, I almost missed the significance of their presence.

Life. I was here to experience it. Standing tall—or as tall as a five-foot-two gal could be—as I levered myself out of the wheelchair. Wearing the tight, constrictive garments tended to pull my shoulders down as well. "Qualifying statements" had become a new mind game as the familiar things that used to be true about my life were different. Nothing seemed as clear-cut or simple anymore. Even a basic task like brushing my teeth had become a multistep, frustrating chore. Eating, dressing, bathing. Every normal task I had taken for granted all my life had to be rethought and redefined. I tried not to dwell on the almost-daily visits I would need back to the burn center for wound care and follow-up for the foreseeable future.

When the car pulled up and Clara opened the door for me to get in, my heart jolted.

The last time I got in a car...

Trying to shake off the thought, I hugged Clara, clung for long seconds, and then gingerly maneuvered myself into the front seat.

I've done this a thousand times. Today's no different.

Our trip was a thirty-minute drive to Murray's condo. My heart raced as the car picked up speed. As we entered into the busy traffic on the City Drive and onto the congested freeway, I willed myself to stay calm and adjust to the feel of the moving vehicle. The cars around us made me nervous. I checked my side mirror for anyone driving too close behind every minute or two. I wished I were the one driving, to feel even a smidgen more of control.

We finally arrived at the complex and pulled up to Murray's two-car garage. I took a deep breath and realized how hot and sweaty I felt after the stressful drive. It was a relief to exit the vehicle. We entered his unit through the enclosed patio. Not having to climb stairs made for an easy though slow walk into the kitchen and family room, the main living space. The bachelor pad was decorated with both old and new art pieces and furnishings. Some were salvaged from his previous home, and some were new purchases marking his fresh start. The master bedroom and bath sat toward the back of the condo. Two small bedrooms were located up a flight of stairs.

Melanie put my things in Murray's room and returned to find me standing in the living room, looking a little lost. The last time I had been at the condo was the day of the car crash. We had played tennis that afternoon and returned to shower and change our clothing for the evening out. It felt good to be back in a familiar environment, out of that sterile, cloying hospital cubicle. Everything in the condo was the same, but I was not the same. Nor would I ever be again. The world seemed off-kilter, and I sensed the adjustment would take all the strength I could muster.

"Barbara, I'm gonna set up your meds next and then get you some lunch. We have to make sure your calorie intake is sufficient."

Melanie's voice brought me back to reality.

"I'm not very hungry..."

She gave me her sergeant look, and I acquiesced.

"Okay. I know. I'll eat."

I sat down at the small round table in the kitchen nook to wait. I couldn't help but think that I would have loved to be sitting at my own kitchen table in my apartment. My friends had thought it prudent to rent it out to relieve me of the financial burden. The saved rent money would come in handy once I was more able to take care of myself and move back in at a later date.

I had to be practical. I simply could not manage to live independently, as much as I wished it were different.

But the feeling of being displaced made me melancholy. My emotions yo-yoed from joy to sadness every three seconds. I told myself I would adjust and focused on the food Melanie placed before me. I hadn't seen or smelled a tuna salad sandwich on whole wheat toast with real mayo for months, and it lifted my mood, my appetite returning. Cut up into tiny pieces because of the tightness of my scarred mouth, the first small bite off my fork made me groan in delight. I vowed to pay attention to simple pleasures as often as possible. The meal ended with banana slices at Melanie's insistence. The potassium supposedly would help my body regain nutritional balance and aid in healing. Not my favorite fruit; I could picture a banana rebellion in the very near future.

"So, what's next?" I asked.

"Why don't you lie down for a while, and later we can do your stretches while we plan out the week?"

Exhausted by the events of the morning, I readily agreed. We slowly walked back into the master bedroom. Melanie helped me take off the Orthoplast mask for an hour break. Every second without it became a moment of freedom. While I was slowly getting used to sleeping with the pressure garments, they were still hot and uncomfortable. It was like being swaddled by two pairs of ultra-tight nylons all over my body.

My thoughts tumbled as I lay down on the king-sized bed and, with care, laid my head on the pillow.

Memories of Murray and me.

Together.

Intimate.

As my eyes closed, I couldn't help but wonder, would he want to hold me again?

* * *

Waking up groggy and out-of-sorts a while later, I got up and walked a few feet to the master bathroom. Flipping on the light with my elbow, I called out, "Melanie, can you help me?"

I held back a groan of annoyance at having to rely on someone else for the simplest of tasks. The tight pressure garments were impossible to take on and off without two functioning hands.

Taking a step into the room, I froze as I came face-to-face with my reflection in the full-length mirror above the vanity. Some caricature from a Hollywood horror film stared back at me. This could not be me. Judy's description of "red and blotchy" did not begin to describe the damage done by the fire.

The only part of my former face I recognized was the color of my eyes. Not a millimeter of my beautiful skin remained. My nose looked like somebody tore the outside tissue away on each side and left only the middle. My upper eyelids were pulled tight, with no eyebrows in sight. The lower lids contracted down, tugging the skin away from the socket. My now-thickened lips stood out huge and twisted, the scars on my chin pulling the lower lip down on one side.

The stark shock of my loss stared back at me. In my worst imaginings, I could not have conjured up this picture. Sheer panic tore me away from the mirror. I bolted screaming from the room and into the living room, circling it around and around until the furniture and walls were a blur, sobbing and continuing to scream.

"I can't live like this. I won't live like this."

Melanie, shocked at my reaction, tried to calm me down.

"Barbara, take a breath. Surely you've seen your face before today. It won't always be like this. Didn't your doctors tell you that?"

I stopped and glared at her. "No! I never could make myself look. I was too afraid. This is beyond fixable. My life is *over*!"

Bawling even harder and more distraught, I brushed past Melanie to get back to the bedroom and slammed the door behind me. I needed to be alone. My heart raced as my thoughts flooded. I walked around the room holding my head, trying to get a handle on the harsh reality.

Why didn't somebody tell me? Prepare me? What the hell were they thinking?

I paced the room in a panic. I cried until nausea set in. Eventually, the shock and despair left a numb fog in their wake. I lay down on the bed and stared at the ceiling.

When Melanie eventually knocked on my door, I allowed myself to be coaxed out of the room. Murray was just arriving home after work, ready to take the night shift for my care. I tried to pull it together for his sake.

He came in with a smile and a plan to celebrate my discharge from the hospital, something I had been looking forward to as well. Instead, I greeted him with tears and reprimands.

"Why didn't you tell me how bad my face looks? Was there some plan to keep me in the dark? By everyone?"

"No, of course not," he said. "Why would you think that? I just assumed you saw your face, honey. I had no idea. You mean they never showed you a mirror?"

"No!" I cried, breaking into tears once again.

"I'm so sorry. You must be in shock. Come here. It's gonna be okay."

He reached out to hug me, and I leaned into him, wrapping my arms around his waist, my face tucked under his chin. I closed my eyes, wishing away a reality beyond my worst nightmares.

After saying goodbye to Melanie and eating a dinner I barely tasted, Murray and I settled on the couch to talk. The doorbell interrupted us, and he jumped up to answer it. Judy had come bearing gifts to welcome me home. She saw how upset I was and sat down with us to hear me out.

"I thought it was like a sunburn, as naïve as that sounds now… that my skin would return to normal," I said, leaning into Murray, shaking my head. "I had no idea how severe the damage was. Everybody is going to stare at me. I can't teach like this…How can I even leave the house like this?"

Judy and Murray looked at each other, as if silently searching for some concrete answer.

Judy attempted to comfort me.

"You've got to be patient and give this time. You've come so far in the last two months. More surgeries can help for sure. It's too early to give up hope for your face. And it's too early to give up hope on your life."

"Judy's right. You haven't even begun plastic surgery to fix the scars. That will change things and help a lot. I've been talking to a friend of mine about the surgeon I mentioned before, Dr. Furnas. He is supposed to be really good. There is hope here, sweetheart. It's going to get better."

Murray let go of my hand and offered to get us something to drink. Judy hugged me close and allowed me to cry. Eventually she showed me the gift she had brought, a new album by Fleetwood Mac called *Rumors*. I asked her to open the package and place the album on the turntable. No one tried to break the silence as the voice of Stevie Nicks flowed over us. The words of one of the songs struck my heart as if the artist wrote them for me.

And what you had...

And what you lost...

* * *

Getting ready for bed took less time than I thought it would. I was already wearing my pajamas, the pressure garments. Murray helped me brush my teeth and put the dreaded white mask back on for the night. While it was okay to take a break from it for an hour or so, I had to be diligent. Especially now that I had seen the mess my face had become. The mask carefully sat over a cotton turban I wore to cover my partially bald head. I had a light cotton robe to wear over my garments, some normal fabric to keep me from feeling like a creature from *Lost in Space*.

Murray took off the robe, helped me settle under the covers, and then got in on the other side of the bed. We took up our normal spooning position, his arm over my waist. His presence comforted me. Emotional exhaustion had taken hold, and I slept soundly for a few hours.

I woke early to a dull throb in my head, thoughts of my new reality pounding their tune. The lyrics from the song floated back through my mind.

And what you had...

And what you lost...

The morning dawned slowly. I watched the darkness turn gray, then light. Unwelcome rays filtered through the curtains, reminding me there was no way to stop this nightmare. No way to stay hidden in the dark. Life would never be the same.

* * *

Arriving at the hospital for outpatient burn care later in the morning, Melanie and I slowly made our way to the burn center. I dreaded the thought of the walk back through the electric doors.

The charge nurse greeted me, "Barbara, back so soon? We haven't even had time to miss ya!"

She called for my nurse, and Melanie took off for the lobby to wait for me. Clara found me and escorted me to the tub room. She helped me undress, starting with the robe that would become the staple piece of my post-hospital wardrobe. It was white and coral, with an abstract floral pattern. With three-quarter-inch flared sleeves, the ankle-length lightweight cotton piece served me well. Clara took off the white mask and peeled off the pressure garments as well. I stepped into a smaller version of the Hubbard tub, one more torture round to tally. The daily outpatient hydro tub baths would be needed for a few more weeks, until all the areas on my body were fully healed. An occupational therapy appointment followed this one. I tried to adjust to the sensation of swirling warm water lightly stinging the wounds. With only a few areas open, the pain level had been greatly reduced compared to my earlier sessions.

"How was your first night back home?" Clara asked.

"It was awful. I saw my face for the first time."

It all hit at once, too many reminders as I sat in the tub. The tears welled up from a deep place. Anger. Despair. Helplessness.

"I hate this place. I hate my life."

My voice rose with each syllable.

"Why did you let me live? *I don't want to live!*"

Clara looked at me wide-eyed, stunned that her formerly compliant and cooperative patient was screaming in anguish. For two and a half months, I had presented like someone coping well with her tragedy, but the coping veil was ripped off, leaving a woman in desperate need of psychological and emotional care.

I scared myself with the keening wails that wouldn't quit. And the violent howling. The point of mental breakdown loomed, and it was all I could do to pull myself back from the edge. I desperately tried to keep my mind from traveling to another dimension from which I feared I would never return.

"I can't do this. I won't do this. I'm not going to do this."

Words of fear and despair kept tumbling out.

Clara stayed calm as several staff members ran into the room, wondering about the screams. The somber faces reflected everyone's concern over my violent reaction. They decided to end the hydro bath early.

"Barbara, take a few deep breaths," Clara said. "Try to get some control back. It's okay to cry. You've probably needed to for a long time. We've been worried about you breaking at some point because you have been too good of a patient, but right now, we need you to calm down so we can get you some help."

Clara finished the bandages as quickly as possible and called for an emergency consult with a therapist on duty at the hospital. Within twenty minutes, my meltdown brought me face-to-face with the head of psychiatry at UCI. He asked me some questions and drew out the story of my injury. He touched gently on the breakdown in the tub room but didn't linger over the details. We talked about my living situation, and I made another appointment with him for the following week. While I didn't feel a connection with him, at least I began to talk about my injury.

None of the burn team had recognized how desperately I needed this. The unit had a social worker, but not a psychologist assigned specifically to deal with mental health concerns. Why wasn't it protocol for a young woman with extensive facial burns and amputations to receive a psychological assessment? It was a question I would be asking for years. A mental health evaluation should be a standard of care for any severe burn.

My emotions were in free fall.

The hard work of psychological recovery had begun.

4

Eye-Opening

We sat in Teresa's cozy office in Anaheim. It had been two months since I had left the hospital, since I had really seen my face for the first time. I sank into the down pillows of her navy and cream chenille sofa, trying to pull my thoughts together.

Teresa, a marriage and family counselor I had known for a decade, faced me in a large upholstered armchair, an ever-present notebook resting on her lap. Her thoughtful blue eyes were framed by wispy long blond hair, compliments of her Dutch farm girl heritage.

The view from the small window lacked inspiration, but seeking out a counselor I knew from before the fire was genius. The hospital psychiatrist had been a disappointment. After three or four sessions, I realized he demonstrated no empathy or seeming care for me as a patient, as a human being. Teresa, while not oozing compassion indiscriminately, empathized deeply with my trauma and drew me out to talk about my inner world.

I was counting on her to help with the profound transition before me, to remake my identity of who I was…to whom I would be. The disconnect between the two had me reeling. I wondered if I would ever find a new normal. Barbara, the social creature who could so easily navigate any and every public setting in the past, now struggling to go anywhere alone unsupported.

Since my accident in February, I had not ventured to a store, restaurant, or even walked down a street without a friend by my side. I was afraid of possible negative encounters and dealing with the stares on my own.

"How are you feeling about Murray?" Teresa asked.

"I'm devastated. Still suffering from the loss of him." The tears welled, and I let them fall. Teresa let me cry.

"Can you tell me what really happened now that you've had time to think about it?"

"I think the surface answer is that he got tired of babysitting me, though I tried to be his partner of old. I would do all my self-care tasks and therapy with Melanie before he got home. I tried to be normal and have regular conversation, to not have everything center around my injury and burn care. I thought we were on a good path. We were intimate a few times, and he seemed to accept my scars."

"And?"

"One night he became really impatient with me. It was one of those nights when I itched constantly and just couldn't get comfortable in the bed. He reamed out at me to stop tossing and turning and to settle down. I was so hurt, I got up and went out to the living room to get away from him. Afterward, we both decided that our living arrangement wasn't working. I moved out the next day to Lynda's apartment, one of my colleagues from school. Murray and I saw each other a few times after that, but then he told me he wanted us to date other people, meaning, of course, that *he* wanted to date other people."

"I'm sorry, Barbara. That had to be very painful to hear. You said on the surface. Does that mean you have a below-the-surface answer for what went wrong?"

"Yeah…He never loved me like I loved him. My friends saw it. They doubted he would stick around long after the fire. I just didn't want to see it."

"So let me ask that question again, how are you *feeling* about Murray?"

"I'm angry—angry that he could so callously abandon me after such a devastating experience and so easily go on to date other people. Does he really think I will be dating anyone anytime soon? How obtuse is the man? And why did all of this happen to me and nothing to him? He gets to be happy and carefree, putting everything behind him practically overnight and move on with his life. It's so unfair. I guess I better enjoy the memories with him because that part of my life is over. No more dancing, parties, tennis, connection! That's how I feel."

I didn't even try to keep the despair out of my voice.

"My heart cries, *he knew me*! If he can't see past my scars to the real me and love me, how will some new man find a way? I feel like my life has fallen to pieces. And the smallest things irritate me. Sudden loud sounds startle and irritate me, tasks I can't do, buttons, zippers, clasps…I'm depressed. I can't sleep. When I finally do, I wake up in a panic and wonder if the accident really happened. Then I feel the tight garments and shadow nerves from my lost fingers, and the sharp reality stuns me."

Teresa bore the brunt of my angst and pain. Our discussions brought all my grief to the surface and left me wiped out. But in the telling and letting myself feel the pain, bricks were being laid, one upon another. My tears moistened the mortar. Perspective shaped the new foundation I was trying to lay for my life. Our weekly sessions gave me a place to start.

* * *

I was back on the cozy sofa two weeks later, ready for the next emotionally grueling session.

Teresa asked me about Catalina Island, and I shared with her the details of my trip from the previous week.

Every July, a group of my closest friends, including Bobby and Judy, ventured to the small island twenty-six miles across the sea from Long Beach. We traveled by boat to work on our tans, play tennis,

47

dance at the Galleon (a local club), and soak up being together. Despite my limitations, I had to go.

We rented five beautiful Spanish-style casitas filled with sturdy rattan furniture and decorated with old Catalina tiles. Painted in adobe colors with a full kitchen, the casitas were located a half mile from downtown. With very few cars on the island, we could walk everywhere. The island had become a family getaway location in the seventies, a safe haven I relished visiting.

With resentment in my heart, I had to invite Melanie along, knowing I wouldn't be able to take care of myself without burdening my friends. It wasn't personal. I was mourning my loss of independence, and she was a constant reminder that everything had been altered in my life.

Melanie helped me prepare for the trip. Finding suitable clothing was no easy task. I had finally relinquished the coral-and-white robe after my occupational therapist confronted me. It took her words to make me realize that depression had been fueling my constant use of the comfy garment. I just hadn't cared. But the Catalina trip mattered to me, and I wanted to be presentable.

We found some lightweight pants and full-length tops that would fit over my pressure garments. A friend sewed a few dresses made from a no-iron crinkly material that were easy to put on and take off. Bandages, creams, salves, and meds took up a huge section of one of my suitcases.

The first day on the island, the sun shone brightly, reflecting off the waters of the bay. The city of Avalon beckoned. Judy knocked on the door of my casita late in the morning, after Melanie had spent several hours helping me with my bath, bandages, garments, and dressing.

"So, what do you wanna do today, Barbara?" Judy asked with her typical grin.

I listed through my head what I really wanted to do: play some tennis, lie in the sun for a couple hours, then jump into the ocean wearing my favorite bikini.

I could do none of those things.

Seeing my lost look, Judy suggested something I could do.

"How about walking downtown for some ice cream?"

Comfort food sounded exactly like what I needed at the moment. We wandered down to our favorite parlor on Crescent Avenue, Lloyd's of Avalon Confectionery. The ocean breeze cooled my pressure garment–clad body as we window-shopped along our path. Having Judy at my side bolstered me.

We finally reached the old-fashioned parlor and wandered in. I eyed the taffy, caramel apples, and colorful homemade suckers begging for attention. They all looked a bit difficult to eat, but no matter as I was here for the luscious ice cream. We headed for the creamy options in the display case, centrally located in the long, narrow shop. Usually I am prone to the purest form of chocolate I can find, but I branched out a little.

"Give me a double scoop of Jamoca almond fudge on a sugar cone."

Judy chose a sorbet, and we walked outside to find a place to sit down. My cone rested between my crooked index finger and left thumb. The first melting drip hit my palm in a matter of seconds. I needed to get busy eating, but the mask limited the movement of my lips and tongue. A small awkward lick gave me the delicious taste I had been craving.

Drip, drip, drip.

My puny efforts couldn't keep up with the melting blob perched precariously in my lopsided left hand. As I tried to shift the angle to reach a new spot, the ice cream plopped to the ground before I could make my stiff fingers begin to react.

I closed my eyes in frustration and fury. Opened them to fling what remained of the cone onto the street for the birds to finish. I burst into tears, humiliated at my failure in the simplest of things.

* * *

The memory hurt. I blinked and focused on Teresa
"I guess you could say it was an eye-opener."
"In what way?" she asked.
I ranted about all the things I couldn't do. And the staring.

"Eyes followed me wherever I went. I saw the double takes, the shocked looks, the whispering and wondering. I felt like a freak. Vacations are supposed to be a break from your problems, right? I just wanted to be normal, out with my friends. They became a buffer. I used them. Clung to them. I couldn't be alone. Oh, how I wanted to close my eyes and wake up normal."

To describe the deep-seated panic of being this other person was beyond me. But I tried to give it words, to express my distress.

Teresa coaxed out my sadness, my struggles.

"Were there any good moments?"

I pondered that one.

"Dancing…Bobby, my dear, sweet Bobby. What a loyal friend. Judy's husband knows how much I love to dance, and he got me out on the floor at the El Galleon, our favorite restaurant, despite the mask and bandages. For those minutes, I felt joy, freedom, a bit of normalcy. I needed that."

"Were people staring at you?"

"I'm sure they were, but I didn't care. I was so caught up in the moment, being in someone's arms and moving to the music. But I don't remember anyone being obnoxious. I think people were trying to be kind."

"So what did you learn from the whole experience?"

"Life will never be the same. Some days I want to end it all… but I can't."

My statement lingered in the air for several moments.

"What stops you?" Teresa asked.

"My mother, mostly. I couldn't do that to her, inflict more loss on her. I am the only one she has left. I have to handle all of this right now on my own."

"Can you?" she asked.

"Handle it? Good question. I'm trying. Having you to vent with helps me. I can't seem to focus on much beyond it. I wake up every morning and just try to motivate myself to get up and do the next thing."

* * *

It was the fall of 1977, seven months after the car crash. I had finally contacted Dr. David Furnas, a highly respected reconstructive surgeon, to begin the improvements to my face. He was the chief of plastic surgery at UCI Medical Center.

My hopes soared sky high that he could work miracles.

"So what is the plan for more surgery?" Teresa wanted to know.

"I see Dr. Furnas this week to discuss a plan. He kind of intimidates me. Deep down, I wonder if he really cares, and I need him to care, ya know? Is that egotistical? I fear I'm just a file in a drawer, another body on his operating table. And I want to be more. What he does will affect my life forever, right?"

"Have you talked to him about this?" Teresa asked. "I think you should."

"Yeah, right. You don't say things like that to doctors! I would feel mortified."

"It may seem risky, I'll grant you that, but it could be really empowering to state your true thoughts and hopes. At least you will know that you expressed your needs. How could that hurt?"

Unconvinced, I continued to balk at Teresa's suggestion to tell him my feelings. But I pondered her words for days to come.

* * *

Walking into the doctor's exam room, I plopped myself up on the paper-covered table, the crinkly sound loud to my ears. I waited with nervous energy for Dr. Furnas to enter. He seemed a giant at over six feet tall, dwarfing my small frame. I loved his kind eyes and the focus he bestowed on my concerns. He was becoming less intimidating as we worked together. We chatted for a few moments, and then I took a deep breath and reached for boldness.

"Dr. Furnas, you are going to have a great impact on my future, and I need to know that I am not just another case to you, not just a folder out of the filing cabinet. I want to matter to you. I need to be important to you."

I gulped in air around the phrases, embarrassing myself with shaking hands and heaving lungs.

Not missing a beat, he gently folded his big arms around me.

"Yes, Barbara," he whispered. "I do care about you, and I am going to do the very best job possible."

I sobbed.

And I believed him.

I pulled out my school staff photo and showed it to him.

"Can you make me look like this again?" I asked.

He studied the picture and then me. He didn't say yes. He didn't say no.

"We will see, Barbara. I promise there will be improvement."

"But can you give me back what I lost?"

"We will try, Barbara. That is all I can tell you."

"But will it ever be the same?" I asked.

"I will do my best to work on your scars."

The belief that he could perform wonders fueled my continued questioning. When I thought of myself, I still pictured the old Barbara: scarless and whole, the woman with the bright smile, delicately curved cupid's bow, and sparkling blue eyes framed by perfect gently tilted lashes. I wanted her back. I couldn't let go and accept the new me.

There is the hope of plastic surgery, and there is the myth of plastic surgery. I hadn't yet figured out the difference between the two. It would prove to be a very tough lesson. Hollywood has long perpetuated the lie that any scar can be fixed with the right surgical technique. But damaged tissue has a stubborn will of its own that no surgical knife can shape perfectly. Those natural and beautiful lines of a person's face are lost forever with a deep burn.

We scheduled the surgery for the middle of November, nine months after the accident. I checked into the hospital the day before and spent the night back on the ward, waking early to pre-op needles and the ride down to the operating room. The medicinal smells hit as they wheeled me into the operating room. They shifted me from the gurney to a hard and narrow table, removing the top part of my hospital gown to stick cold electrodes on my torso for the heart monitor.

"A gal could get frostbite in here," I said, just as Dr. Furnas walked through the door. I breathed easier to see his concerned eyes.

"Barbara, are you causing trouble? Let's put on your favorite George Winston cassette so you can relax, and we'll begin our work."

He leaned over me and held on to both of my shoulders as the anesthesiologist inserted the IV, followed by the medication to put me to sleep. His eyes never left mine. A feeling of security washed over me.

"Okay, Dr. Furnas, do a good job, please."

The room began to fade.

"Don't worry, Barbara. We'll take good care..."

* * *

Five days later, I was still in the hospital awaiting the first bandage change after the surgery. Waking up every morning in one of the old cloying cubicles with the smells and sounds triggering trauma memories had taken a fair amount of emotional energy. I felt a sad sense of regression. My upper thigh donor site area stung like mad, though slowly healing. Robbing Peter to pay Paul, some of my good skin had to be sacrificed in the form of a second-degree burn to be used for the reconstruction process. A layer of skin had been removed with a surgical instrument that looked like a large mechanical razor blade. The skin was then surgically placed on my upper lip, lower cheek, and chin using minute stitches to fasten it in place.

Time had been crawling by, measured by the *drip, drip, drip* of the antibiotic fluids flowing into my bloodstream from the bag hanging next to my bed.

My sole focus was to manage the pain and anxiety post-surgery.

Dr. Furnas appeared in my doorway. I was glad to see him, but also dreading the bandage removal to see the results of his work. He gently began to remove the gauze from the new grafts on my face. Layer after layer peeled away. I had high hopes that some of my former image had been restored.

As the last of the bandages fell to the bed, Dr. Furnas handed me a mirror. "Well, Barbara, I think the site looks good. You have a perfect take here with the new sheet grafts. I'm very pleased."

Looking at the new red skin, I tried to see what he saw and stay positive, but failed abysmally.

"Okay…but why is there such a big space between my upper lip and nose? Before, that part of my face was half the size. It looks so out of proportion. Who has that kind of dimension on their face?"

"I've left room for contractures. As the graft matures, it will shrink a bit, hopefully making just the right amount of skin to look normal."

I nodded my head, hiding the dismay.

The disappointment.

"And how long will that take?" I asked.

"Let's give this particular graft nine months with some form of pressure, and then see," he said. "We can always go back and make some minor adjustments. In the meantime, we can start working on other areas."

Long after he left, I stared at what I had thought would be my new beautiful upper lip. All I saw was a distorted, elongated, and shapeless graft. The bitter thought that I belonged in a primate hospital until the graft matured made me slam the mirror down on the bed. With my eyes closed, I lay there taking slow deep breaths. The tears welled up and seeped out. The image of my upper lip lingered. My hope of getting my face back had been shattered.

* * *

Teresa listened to my bitter disappointment with the first reconstructive surgery by Dr. Furnas.

"My face is gone forever," I said. "I get that now. I had such hope. Now I see how stupid I was to believe everyone's talk of oh-wait-and-see-how-much-plastic-surgery-can-do. What a joke."

"I'm sorry, Barbara. That has to be incredibly hard to accept. I think you're going to have to give yourself a lot of time and space to process it. Do you feel like you are doing that?"

"If you're asking if I'm being honest with myself, then yes, I am. I cry a lot, and the weight of it never leaves me…It's hard to describe…It feels like a death of some kind, and I'm in mourning. A part of me is missing, gone forever…And the hardest thing is that I have no idea what the final result will be. I've gone from wanting my old face back to just wanting to look good enough that people won't stare at me out in public. And that is not a given."

"Grief is one of those strange beasts that has tentacles everywhere. I don't mean this to sound like a platitude, but it's really important that you are being honest with yourself, and I commend you for it."

Though I was thankful I could pour out my feelings to Teresa, I left her office with a heavy heart. I didn't know what my future would look like. Or what I would look like.

* * *

Two months later, Teresa helped prepare me for the next phase of reconstruction. While my expectations had been lowered, I hadn't given up hope for a measure of more improvement. I couldn't. My life and my future rested on moving forward.

"The next surgery will be on my nose and reconstructing the nostrils. Dr. Furnas suggested using my big toe as a donor. He wants to use the fleshy part at the base, which means there wouldn't be much left of it afterward. He would have to amputate it," I said, looking down at my perfect, unburned feet, nails lacquered a bright red and encased in cute sandals.

Having already lost so many fingers, I was appalled at the idea.

"I started crying and told him that I couldn't lose any more body parts."

"How did he respond?" Teresa asked.

"He just nodded and thought for a minute. He said he would come up with a plan B."

His sensitivity made him stand out as a surgeon who didn't just care about cutting. He saw beyond the physical to my deep-seated emotions, balancing truth with sensitivity to keep me motivated to pursue recovery.

"He is going to use the tips of my ears to rebuild the lost nostrils. He says he can mold and shape them to create a straight look, in harmony with my face."

The fatherlike care he showed me mattered. Dr. Furnas understood that my body image had been shattered, and he could significantly shape my new identity. Giving me some control over the plans and taking the time to answer my endless questions helped me immensely.

"I couldn't ask for a better surgeon—a better person to be in charge of my care. I just wish he could perform miracles. I miss seeing me in the mirror. I want it all back—my nice skin, the natural lines of my face, my smile. I can still hardly believe it's all gone."

I had come face-to-face with my losses. I had to let go of the old Barbara. Denial for a time may have kept me from complete despair. But in the long run, closing my eyes to reality would trap me in the past with only bitterness in my future.

I felt fortunate to have people loyal to me on this journey—my mother and my aunt, colleagues with whom I taught, my friends both near and far. Several of my students visited over the summer. I had Teresa, prayer groups, hospital staff, and therapists all cheering me on. It was both humbling and encouraging to realize how many people cared about me. If there was a bright light to any of this, it was getting a glimpse of that love from others. It fostered a strength I didn't know I had to keep moving forward, to accept this new me. I couldn't do it alone. I couldn't rebuild my life and my identity by myself.

No one should have to try.

5

Revelations

"**B**arbara, we are taking you out to dinner. Be ready at six thirty," Judy said cheerfully through the phone line.

A year or so after my car crash, Bobby and Judy knew that a social life mattered to me. They continued to drag me out of the apartment I shared with my friend Lynda. After Murray and I had officially ended, my Saturday nights were lonely. I consoled myself with the thought that my accident tested our relationship and discovered its weaknesses. But the sadness I felt went deep. I truly wondered if I would ever have another relationship, a man to hold my hand, kiss me, and make love to me. Part of my identity had always been defined in some way by being with someone. The idea of creating this new life alone was new territory. My good friends understood my fears.

"I'll be ready, Judy. Casual or dressy?"

"No evening gowns for sure…casual," she replied.

I stood in front of the mirror prepping for the evening. My hair was growing back oh so slowly. The need for a temporary wig remained. The grafts on my forehead and upper cheeks had become flatter and whiter from faithfully wearing the Orthoplast mask for so many months. The area looked like a poorly designed patchwork quilt, the grafts pieced together. I wished for perfectly smooth skin, all one tone—my former skin.

The new grafts on my upper lip and chin appeared blotchy red, but were an improvement over the raised red scar lines of the recent pre-surgery look. A new bump on my upper lip had me worried. My beautiful cupid's bow was a distant memory. I couldn't help but desire that some of this could be fixed with the next surgery, but down deep, a desperate fear churned. Every time I looked at myself, the naïve belief that Dr. Furnas could restore any semblance of my former appearance slipped farther off the shelf of lingering hope.

Having graduated from the large white Orthoplast contraption, my new tan cloth chin strap replaced the mask. It covered my lower cheeks, upper lip, and chin, leaving my newly repaired nose free to heal. I told the mask to do a better job. I wished it would listen. The partial hairpiece came next. I stared at my reflection. Shook my head. The mirror ignored my scolding-teacher look.

I was being forced to reinvent myself, one revelation at a time.

I realized that as a woman in my early thirties, I had often relied on being cute and flippant in my interactions with the world. But I was not that girl any more. "Cute" was gone, though "flip" I could still do pretty well if given the chance. Small comfort. Cute worked for me. I wanted it back.

* * *

Bobby, Judy, and I walked into a Marie Callender's restaurant packed with diners. My friends wanted to give me a taste of normalcy, a simple outing, the kind I had always taken for granted. The hostess called our name, and we moved toward our waitress to follow her to a back table. I felt the stares from every direction. I set my eyes forward and focused on the back of the restaurant.

The brown mask screamed, "Look at me!"

Bobby whispered, "Chin up. Shoulders back. Walk like you own the place."

My heart pounded, but I followed his advice. It didn't lessen the staring, but I felt a smidgen of control. The pain of the unwanted attention didn't outweigh the magnitude of my need for a social life. I counted the cost and made a pact with myself to not let it stop me despite the anxiety. But the unpredictability of the public put me on edge constantly. Leaving the house posed a risk. Every single time.

* * *

The buddy system saved me more than once.

My roommate Lynda and I ventured out one January evening, almost a year after the accident. Lynda and I were colleagues from my junior high school. She taught French in the classroom next to mine. Lynda had an athletic build and blondish-brown hair with a short, wavy cut. Blue eyes and a beautiful smile enhanced her all-American-girl look. She turned out to be a caring roommate but not a coddling one, just what I needed to grow in independence and do more things for myself as the weeks and months went by.

We were catching up over margaritas at a Mexican restaurant. Waiting in the bar area for a table in the dining area, I noticed a gentleman staring at me from a barstool. Catching my eye, he teasingly shouted, "Hey! Halloween's been over for months. You can take your mask off."

When we attempted to ignore him, he yelled a little louder, "Hey! What's with the mask?"

Not getting any response, he got up to find out why we were acting so unsocial.

"Brace yourself," Lynda said.

I watched the man stop dead in his tracks a few feet away as he realized my mask had nothing to do with Halloween.

His eyes popped, and his cheeks took on the hue of cooling lava.

"Oh my gosh, I'm such an idiot. Please forgive me for bugging you and making a fool of myself. I'm so sorry—I wasn't thinking—I…"

"It's okay. Don't worry about it," Lynda piped in. "It's a medical thing. We're fine. We understand. Have a good night."

She nodded and turned her eyes back to me after the attempt to soothe his ruffled feathers, shooing him away from us.

My feathers were about to molt.

He mumbled a few more words as he hurried out of the bar, waving a last apology and shaking his head, lava cheeks still aglow.

We both looked at each other and sighed.

"That's gonna cost me at least a couple of sessions with Teresa," I said.

"I'm really sorry, Barbara. Someday we'll laugh about it. You are going to have to be incredibly strong when you go out and about. People react without thinking."

Lynda attempted to console me, and I was thankful for her presence and perspective. I needed to get better at this. But I feared the cost would take its toll and isolate me over time. The emotional energy it took to rescue interactions in public made me choose carefully my social outings.

Sometimes I was more self-conscious about my hands than my face. I envied my friends with their perfectly straight fingers and long manicured nails. They took them for granted, something I could never, ever do. Judy would often scratch my back over the pressure garments during one of my incessant itching fits. It grieved me to see her lovely hands and remember my former normalcy. I tried to explain it to my occupational therapist.

"My dad had beautiful hands. Mine were a smaller, more delicate version, and I took pride in them. I enjoyed manicures and polishing my nails on a regular basis. Now, I just don't know what to do with them..." I held up my right hand—small, stubby, and fingerless—to make my point.

"I can't even pretend to imagine what that is like, Barbara. I wish I could give them back to you...but here's an idea. Have you ever considered prosthetic hands? I know that some people use them. Maybe we could have some special ones made. Would that help you feel less self-conscious? They will only be semi-functional, but from a distance, they could look fairly natural," she said.

The idea intrigued me. Living near Hollywood afforded me access to resources a lot of the survivor world couldn't tap into so readily. We decided to go ahead with the plan. Judy and I searched the phone book to track down a company that would be willing to help me. We found one in West Los Angeles. I made numerous trips to a small special effects studio located in a strip mall to complete what turned out to be a long process.

For the first phase, one of the artists, Peyton Massey, a stocky man with kind blue eyes red hair sprinkled with gray, took a mold of my hands. He then searched for a female hand model to match the general size and shape of them. The second phase involved creating the prostheses from latex and painting them just the right color to match the skin of my arms for authenticity. Months of prep work and multiple visits for color matching were needed to keep the process moving forward.

Like a pregnant mom, I waited with great anticipation the nine months that it took for the custom hands to be made. Their arrival brought me great joy.

I rushed down to the studio when I received the phone call. Peyton came out to greet me. He was in his fifties, and passion for his work came across in his exuberance.

"Barbara, come on back. I know it's taken a stretch of time for us to finish your hands, but I think you're gonna be very pleased with the result."

He escorted me to his workroom where a long table full of tools and molds of projects at various stages occupied most of the space. A light layer of plaster of Paris dust covered the surface. He sat me down for the reveal. Gently pulling the prostheses from a plastic box, my first glimpse of the end result thrilled me.

"Peyton, they are so pretty and elegant. I love how real they look," I said.

Smiling, he helped me put the remainder of my right hand into the right base, zipping the enclosure tightly up the underside of my wrist to just below the elbow. The latex was soft, and I could manipulate the fingers to position them. For the opposite hand, my slightly crooked left fingers flowed into the latex like a tight glove, with a similar zipper to keep the piece in place.

They looked beautiful. I now had matching fingernails on both hands, painted a deep rose color that was feminine and appealing. I knew they weren't real. But they made me feel a semblance of normalcy I hadn't experienced for over a year.

I had a wedding to attend and decided to take my new hands for a spin. I donned a sapphire blue two-piece suit with a fitted waist and long sleeves. Going anywhere alone still posed a problem for me. This was a big Italian wedding, and I only knew the bride, one of my favorite former students, and her family. Walking into a group with at least a few familiar faces eased my anxiety, though showing up alone forced me to interact with a fair number of strangers. But even though I was uncomfortable, I couldn't just sit in a chair like a log all night. My social self really wanted to engage with others, so I looked for people who seemed approachable. The reception took place in an elegantly decorated ballroom. As I waited in line for a plate of appetizers, a forty-something man introduced himself.

"Hi. I'm Tony, the bride's favorite uncle. Wasn't she just gorgeous today?" he asked, holding out his hand to shake mine, smiling broadly. "Do you know the bride or the groom?"

"The bride. I was her junior high English teacher."

As I spoke, I placed my right hand in his. Instead of the normal squeeze-and-shake motion, he faltered when he felt the odd texture. All motion stopped for a long moment. He quickly released the prosthesis. My face heated up, and I wasn't sure what to say. Neither one of us addressed the obvious.

"Have you tasted the wine yet?" he asked. His eyes flitted away awkwardly and shifted back, focusing slightly to my left. "Try the red. I bet it pairs nicely with the Italian meatballs…"

He turned to the person behind him and struck up another conversation.

I shook off the encounter and continued through the line. I balanced the luncheon-size plate on the right prosthetic, spooning food onto it with my left hand. With careful concentration, I managed to add a few items and walked over to a table to sit down.

I breathed a sigh of relief. The prosthetic hands forced me to think through each action I had to face ahead of time. I discovered I could use a fork and knife in a semi-normal fashion. I could lift my glass of wine easily for the toasts to the bride and groom. Clapping sounded funny with the latex material, but with discreet movements, I gave the appearance of daintily putting my hands together to cheer on the father-and-daughter dance.

I didn't attempt to open the party favor chocolates sitting in front of my plate. Nor could I open the ribbon-clad nylon bags of seed to throw at the bride and groom as they took off for their honeymoon. Intricate manipulations required more movement than the prostheses were capable of.

While I loved my new hands at a distance, close encounters and certain actions continued to cause problems and uncomfortable moments. I had to carefully think through each step of an outing to decide if the hands would help or hinder. I learned the hard way that traveling by plane posed several dilemmas I struggled to overcome, such as reaching into my handbag for my boarding pass, buckling my seat belt, and tearing open a bag of peanuts. While I was fine with asking for help in a pinch, my fierce sense of independence demanded I conquer these actions on my own. While stubbornness was a good thing that in many ways had brought me this far, it could also hinder me.

After a couple months of experiments with the prosthetic hands for social outings, my dissatisfaction with them grew. I hadn't anticipated the awkward moments, the lack of functionality, and the curiosity sometimes raised by the prostheses.

It dawned on me over a period of time that I would rather have people know the real me. Hiding created speculation that had to be dealt with at some point. I learned that hiding my hands in my pockets was futile. I couldn't fool people for long. Eventually I would have to use them to do something, making the stares even worse. Wouldn't it be better to just get it over with right from the first encounter? People might be shocked at the first meeting, but they would get past it. And then I would be free to be me. Being self-conscious about my hands probably drew more attention with furtive movements and awkward body language than if I just acted completely normal about their appearance. And to have to wear long sleeves in a hot, dry climate to hide the prostheses also posed problems for my fashion taste, let alone comfort.

What had seemed a creative fix to my lost hands was no longer viable. I carefully wrapped them up in tissue paper and placed them in the bottom drawer of my dresser. Time to face reality. My beautiful hands were gone. Nothing could ever give them back to me or make the loss less profound. I chose to let the world see me as I am.

My next revelation came at another wedding. A dear friend had found a partner, and I couldn't miss the celebration. I chose a new fancy dress and left the prosthetic hands at home. The reception was held at a swank hotel in Orange County. This time I had Bobby and Judy with me, making the evening a relaxing one. A local band started to warm up, and it put a smile on my face.

A man named Jerry introduced himself and asked me to dance to the song "Reunited" by Peaches & Herb. I happily agreed. Taking me in his arms, he awkwardly grabbed low on my right wrist, holding my little appendage bobbing up and down for all to stare at. It mortified me, and I felt everyone had to be staring at my little hand. After a couple turns around the dance floor, I decided I had to do something.

"Jerry, it's okay for you to hold on to my hand directly. It won't hurt me."

I tugged my hand down into his palm, and his long fingers closed around it.

"Oh…I didn't know if your hand was sensitive. Sorry…uh… thanks for telling me," he said.

His sheepish look told me a lot. He really hadn't known what to do. I applauded him asking me to dance in the first place with my mask and pressure garments. Boldly having to rescue the many awkward social moments I face wore on me, but this was now a part of my life. My teaching skills had to extend far beyond the classroom and into my daily encounters.

Always the teacher.

But what about the lover in me?

A real relationship seemed so far out of reach. If I can't even share a normal dance with a man, how could I expect a marriage? My facial difference, my hands, the scars on my body. Could anyone accept the new me?

My first solo outing to a mall had to eventually take place. It came on a weekday, a year and a half after the car accident. None of my go-to friends could get away to make the run with me. A colleague's birthday was coming soon, and I wanted to buy a gift. I sat in my apartment to gather courage and planned my route to the upscale Fashion Island in Newport Beach. Getting into my car gave me a little thrill of freedom. As promised by Dr. Klein, my right hand had a space between the base of what used to be my thumb and forefinger, allowing me to grip on to the steering wheel. My left hand clung to the side of the wheel in guide mode. Not having to shift gears saved me. Thank goodness for automatic transmissions.

I parked near Bullocks Department Store, entered quickly, and wandered through the clothing section. Not having a buddy near for distraction purposes had me looking around and noticing other shoppers glancing at me. Double glancing at me. I didn't look too closely for any triple takes. Instead, I tried to focus on my task.

Remember the goal. Get in, make a selection, pay, and get out.

I came across a sweet soft rose cardigan that seemed perfect for my friend. The price wasn't bad.

The nearest checkout counter stood a few feet away. I presented my purchase to the clerk—a fifty-something, smartly dressed, serious-looking woman who seemed all business—and fumbled to get the wallet out of my purse. Her eyes followed my every move, glanced at the mask, and back down to my hands. I could guess her thoughts: *Isn't it a pity?*

Smiling and looking her in the eye, I started chatting. "How is your day going? I just love this sweater, and it will look so cute on my friend, who has beautiful blonde hair and brown eyes… and at such a good price…"

Her expression changed. Warmth sprung up as she smiled and responded to my comments. It helped us both feel more comfortable. I managed to pay and grasp the package from her hands.

"It was a pleasure to wait on you, and I hope you have a good day. Thanks for coming in," she said with a smile.

I smiled back and exited the store. I took a deep breath, relieved and a tad triumphant. Maybe strangers would feel pity when they saw my mask and hands, but I was *not* going to act like I deserved pity. Or that I was pitiful. Just the opposite. Maybe it would make a difference. The double takes wouldn't go away anytime soon. If I could learn to feel a measure of control in risky social situations, so much the better for me.

Lying in bed that night, I pondered the recent revelations that had come my way. To think of rescuing a lifetime of social interactions exhausted me. Knowing I had to continually put others at ease would take emotional energy, a gracious attitude, and fortitude. Some days I wouldn't be up to the task. Some days I would want to drown in my own self-pity parties. The unfairness and the reality of it kept my eyes open, staring into the dark.

I was the one hurt. Yet I am the one who has to do all the work, helping people over my scars...

A hard truth. Spoken softly to myself. I couldn't survive on cute and flip. A deeper reality had to be called upon to rebuild my life. I despaired that I might lack the strength. But I knew down deep I had the determination.

My life was too precious to waste.

6

Reentry

Fourteen long months after my accident, I was finally ready to live independently. My apartment had been subleased and saved for me, but my physical limitations and the memories, the mourning of my former life, kept me from wanting to return to it.

I now wanted a new start.

I had to regain a sense of safety.

My hand limitations gave me a feeling of vulnerability that had to be compensated for. I chose to buy a condo in Seal Beach. It was located in a secure complex with subterranean parking and a push-button electric garage door. With only fifty-four units on a quiet tree-lined street, the complex felt neighborly and safe. I had a unit on the second floor with two bedrooms and two-and-a-half bathrooms overlooking the pool.

Finally I was surrounded by my own art and furnishings, used my own dinnerware, and slept in my own bed with my favorite set of sheets and pillows. I had missed these comforting elements of my former life. They signaled a step toward true independence and a new integrated identity, for which I longed. Though some things were the same in my life, I had to create a new normal.

I daydreamed about being an English teacher again. The memories flowed: the special connections, the smiles, even the whining about writing "perfect paragraphs."

"Seriously, Miss K? You're torturing us with this writing stuff."

"What's with all the red lines on this page? It's how I talk..."

Junior high kids were like young artists just beginning to paint their own lives. And I got to influence texture, color, style.

I missed them. I missed my colleagues. I missed having a purpose for getting out of bed in the morning. Being left behind, out of the game of life, scared me the most. I needed to be a player, to contribute something worthwhile to humanity, no matter how insignificant it may seem. Everyone does.

For the last year and a half, I had been on the receiving end, relying on a team of people to help prod me toward recovery. It was time for me to reengage with the world, but I wondered if the world wanted to reengage with me. Specifically, could my junior high students, not known for their sensitivity, handle a one-handed, mask-wearing, scarred, five-feet-of-pressure-garment-clad burn survivor as their teacher?

My school, Orangeview Junior High in Anaheim, and the district administration had been very supportive after my injury. Many of the staff urged me to return. My network of spies, however, told a different story. Wanting to protect me, some wondered if I should choose a different career, one out of the spotlight.

In the 1970s, it was more normal than not for people with a visible burn injury to become isolated and permanently disabled. Initially, the principal probably figured that I would never return to work as an educator.

The first time some kid yelled, "Hey, there is that ugly burned teacher" in the hallway, the mortification would destroy me. Or so the theory went.

It worried me too. But the plans had been set in motion. And I needed a job. I was my sole support.

A month before the fall semester of 1978 began, I made a panic call to Lynda, my former colleague with whom I shared a love of France and happy hours. In this age before texting, we used to pass notes back and forth, using our students as couriers.

Drinks? 5:00. Meet in parking lot.

I needed it all to be the same, the camaraderie and the normalcy. The panic had been stealthily creeping up on me. Lynda had decided to change schools. She accepted a job as a counselor at another school in our district, Pine Junior High in Los Alamitos. I wanted her to be back in the classroom next to mine to help ease my reentry. But that wasn't possible.

"Lynda, how can I make this work? My new kids will freak. I will freak 'cause they are freaking. I can't do it!"

My imagination ran wild. I pictured an out-of-control classroom with me frozen by the chalkboard, hyperventilating.

"Barbara, take a breath. And don't panic. You just have to be yourself and let the real you shine through. Your students will get used to the new Miss K., and they will love you. I know it."

"I wish it were that simple. I could get another job—hide away in some corporate cubicle. No one would have to deal with me, nor I with them…" My voice trailed off, still rumbly from my panic attack.

"Wait a minute. Since when did you become so insecure, afraid of the world? You haven't come this far to run away and hide. You're stronger than you think. You survived that wretched crash for a reason. And all of those reconstruction surgeries. I know you can do this!"

"But what if I can't?"

"Barbara, do you remember the first time I visited you in the hospital?"

"Vaguely. Parts of those first few weeks are pretty hazy, but I do remember one long conversation late one evening."

"Yes. We talked about the possible meaning of your crash, that through it all, something good could come out of all the pain. I still believe that. And if you hide away for the rest of your life, you could stifle the good."

We talked a while longer, and it helped me to rally, but I still groaned as I hung up the phone. There had to be a plan for my reentry back to school, some way for me to feel more in control of my destiny. Surely I was not the first person to have walked this road?

I called the burn center to ask if they had any ideas. A long stream of patients had gone before me. A professional there had to have some advice. After hemming and hawing for a few minutes, the charge nurse on the other end said they didn't have any resources for this sort of situation.

I was on my own.

A support group gathered at my burn center once a month. It provided information and talk time for survivors and their families, a space to share concerns and challenges.

I was only two weeks away from my classroom debut. I thought maybe my fellow survivors would have some ideas for me. I arrived a little early at the hospital to help set up and greet the attendees. The familiar smells hit me as I entered the burn unit, a cloying mix of disinfectant, bandages, and other odors wafting from patient cubicles. I walked down the corridor away from the memories to the main conference room near the nurses' lounge. The survivors arrived one or two at a time, until most of the seats around the table were filled.

We began with a check-in.

"Hi. I'm Shirley, one of the occupational therapists on the unit, and I'm glad you all could make it. Let's go around the room. Tell us a bit about yourself, how you're doing, and what's new."

She signaled for the person on her right to start, a broad-shouldered man in his fifties with long gray hair gathered in a ponytail.

"Hi, I'm Brad. I crashed my little Piper Cub a few years back in bad weather—was lucky to get out alive. After twenty surgeries and months of rehab, I went back to flying—minus a few fingers—but that doesn't hold me back." He held up his right hand, wiggling the digits he had left with a grin on his slightly scarred face. "News for me? My daughter's gettin' married next month. I'm one proud daddy."

Several people called out their congratulations, and we moved on to the next person.

"Hello, my name is Gina, and I just got out of the hospital. I had a cooking accident in my kitchen apartment on campus. None of my roommates were around to help me put out the oil fire on the stove, and it caught my shirt on fire. My face, arms, and chest got it pretty bad."

A collective groan went up from the group, heads nodding in empathy.

"I'm really scared about the future. How will the other students react to me? I don't know if I can keep up academically with all of the therapy and itching, plus the future surgeries I will need. I want to get back to school so badly, but I feel like my life is on hold."

The next gentleman at the table introduced himself, until everyone had a chance to share.

I ended the check-in.

"Hi. I'm Barbara, and I was burned twenty-one months ago in a car accident. I have some big news. In two weeks, I will be back in the classroom teaching again for the first time. I'm excited but also panicky. I have no idea how my students will react to me. Anybody have any advice?"

"Besides, 'Beam me up, Scotty?'" someone joked. "No!"

"Man, you are one brave woman! I don't know what I would do in your shoes. Probably just bluff my way through, pretend everything was normal," Brad said.

"I wanna say, just be yourself. But that probably isn't very helpful," another confided. No one else ventured forth anything concrete or brilliant that I could use.

Just be myself.

Not bad advice, but I still needed a plan.

We moved on to the night's topic. A representative from the Jobst pressure garment company brought a presentation to show the newbies. I owned up to a love-hate relationship with the tight cloth pieces. I would ditch them in a heartbeat, but having additional surgeries on my face forced me to keep wearing the full-body garments and the mask. The scars on my back and arms still showed signs of

71

thickness that I wanted to keep under control. The Jobst garments offered the best hope.

The rep showed a film depicting the numerous benefits of the specialized clothing. It described what a burn scar looked like and how it matured over time. It showed the results that could occur if one didn't consistently wear them. I liked the simplicity of the information shown, and I realized this film could be a tool for my reentry. My kids could see what a scar looked like without me having to show them my own. I was far too insecure to flash my "designer skin." The fear lingered that one of them would look at me and say, "Yuck!" or "Sick!" It would devastate me. The representative agreed to lend me a copy.

A plan was forming.

*   *   *

I woke up early on the first day of school. Excitement and dread blended together as my nurse arrived early to help me get ready. The daily ritual of bathing and applying and rubbing several layers of cream into my skin, along with tugging on the tight-fitting garments, remained something I could not do alone. Melanie helped me put on lightweight slacks to camouflage the pressure garments and a loose-fitting long-sleeved top for coolness and comfort.

Dressed in teacher attire for the first time since the accident, I sat at my table and sipped a much-needed cup of coffee, reflecting. A new school year was about to start, with kids in new clothes, carrying fresh notebooks and sharpened pencils. There would be a buzz in the air as eighth and ninth graders greeted one another. Lost seventh graders would be wandering the halls trying to find their way into my classroom for the first period. I reminded myself to breathe.

How will the new me fit into the mix? What can I do to make this day less of a threatening disaster?

I decided on honesty. I wondered if complete self-disclosure would pave the way for them to understand what I had been through. Maybe I could change my students' possible pity into empathy.

I ran into Mickey, an English teacher whose classroom sat two doors down from mine, in the half-empty parking lot, and we walked in together. I thought it would be a good idea to arrive early. The familiar sights and smells brought quick tears, but I swallowed them back. Today was a good day. A triumphant one. And I needed to focus on that.

Mickey walked me to my room and gave me a hug for good luck. "You are going to do well. The kids will be fine. Pass a note if you need me," she whispered with a smile. "With Lynda gone, just remember I'm here for you."

Mickey's words gave me courage. I felt the weight of being a teacher again, of needing to set a good example. Teachers were held in high esteem in the seventies, set on a pedestal in many ways. We were mortified to be caught drinking a cocktail at a restaurant or, heaven forbid, smoking a cigarette. Mickey hid her cigarettes in a metal Band-Aid box in her purse, just in case a student peeked in. It was as if we had no flaws or normal lives to our students. I had a reputation to uphold.

After organizing my room, I sat on a stool up at the front on full display as my new students trickled in. I greeted them one by one, took their names, and seated them in alphabetical order. Several eyed me warily, but they obeyed my missives. My new students sat quietly, partially from not knowing each other but probably also from wondering about my appearance.

I handed out books and planning sheets and performed the normal first-class tasks. We would be reading *The Diary of Anne Frank* for our first literature piece. For each chapter, my students would have to write a summary with their impressions of the plot and themes. No one commented on my hands, but I noticed them noticing as I set a book on each desk.

Sitting back on my stool, I looked up, smiled, and began.

"I know you're all probably wondering why I'm wearing a mask and these brown garments. Well, twenty-one months ago, I was involved in a car crash…"

I shared with them the fiery details of my story and my valiant rescue, about my time at the burn center and the new skin grafts. The film from the Jobst company gave them some visuals and additional information, confirming the benefits of wearing the tight garb. I also talked about the upcoming surgeries I would have to undergo, wanting them to be prepared for the fact that my time in the classroom could be interrupted. I then invited them to throw the too-afraid-to-ever-ask questions at me, whatever they wanted to know. My only stipulation was that my weight and age were off-limits.

A student in the back row braved the first one. "Are you ever going to look like you used to?"

"Well, I will be having more surgeries in the coming months, but I won't ever look exactly like I used to. There was just too much damage. But I hope they can get close."

A girl from somewhere in the middle piped in. "Why are the fingers on your left hand so crooked?"

"The joints were very damaged and just won't straighten or bend properly," I responded.

"Can you drive a car?"

"Sure. I will be driving back and forth to school every day. See this little grip area?" I asked, holding up my right hand with the thumb-like pincher. "I can use it to grasp the wheel quite nicely."

"Cool!" said a boy from the front row. A group of kids nodded. Others sat with lowered eyebrows, looking at their own hands, curious what having a hand similar to mine would be like.

I went to the board and wrote my name with beautiful cursive letters.

"Wow! How do you do that with no fingers?" the same boy asked.

"You know…It's not what you have. It's what you do with what you have," I responded. "Just think what awesome penmanship you could have with all of your fingers."

He nodded thoughtfully.

"Any other questions?"

"Does your skin still hurt?" a girl from the front row asked.

"No, it doesn't hurt. But sometimes it feels kind of tight. And itchy," I said.

By the end of my sharing time, the atmosphere had changed. The uneasy quiet had been replaced by a new level of acceptance and understanding. Speaking aloud what most likely would have been left unsaid took away the fear, the mystery, and the sense of being uncomfortable to broach the subject. I pulled the rug out from under their feet, and they didn't even realize it.

Before the bell rang, I made a suggestion.

"You know what? I could use your help. There are lots of kids walking around school today who don't know what you kids know. They will be wondering why I'm wearing these unique garments. You can be my spokespersons out there, helping other students understand. Do you think you can do that for me?"

The bell sounded. Before I dismissed my students, several nodded their heads in agreement. Afterward, the kids jumped up to rush out the door, but a few lingered.

"I'll help, Ms. Kammerer. Thanks for sharing."

"I'm glad you told us. I'll be a spokesperson," another said.

"See you tomorrow, Miss K!"

One classroom down. Five more to go. The eighth graders and ninth graders came next. I wondered if they would be as compassionate.

By 3:15 p.m., I was exhausted but relieved the long day was behind me and ready for one of those happy-hour rendezvous with Lynda. We ended up at a local watering hole to debrief.

"So, here's to your first day in a classroom again," Lynda said, clinking my wineglass with her own. "How are you feeling? How did our not-so-savvy seventh graders respond?"

"Surprisingly well! On both counts. Thank you so much for your support...I wasn't sure I could pull this off!"

"You are back! You took a huge risk. I'm proud of you," Lynda said, giving me the I-knew-you-could-do-it look.

I smiled my slightly crooked smile.

"One of my eighth graders must be a little accident prone," said Lynda. "He cut his finger within five minutes of walking in the classroom. Don't ask me how. He must know some French because I heard him cursing under his breath and had to send him to the principal's office for being rude—that is, after a stop at the nurses' station."

"How do you know the curse words?" I asked.

"I dated a French sailor. He was such a hunk!"

We talked about our new students, the bright, the quirky, and the strugglers. We planned our semester and our get-away strategies. I loved the focus, the laughter, and the satisfaction of a day well spent back in a beloved environment.

As I sipped the last of my wine, a thought struck me: by hiding, we give away power, but by disclosing, we can take it back. It would be too easy to shy away from public arenas like markets, kids' games, movie theaters, churches, and restaurants. But if I did that, I would give others control of my life. I would give power to people I did not know and may never know. What I feared they might think of me would suddenly become more important than what I thought of myself. I didn't want others to dictate my life. I was beginning to understand that I could retain power in social situations by being up-front, honest, and confident. I realized that the power of self-disclosure could really set me free.

And being at work every day gave me much: a schedule, a purpose, accountability, normalcy. I felt more whole. I fit in. I was taking a huge piece of my life back after the accident. My identity had to center on the real me, far deeper than my scars. Living with a body difference didn't mean I *was* the body difference.

My dreams mattered, and they were not so outside of my reach.

7

Faltering Steps

When another school in the district, Pine Junior High, recruited me to teach for them, I decided to change locations in the middle of my first academic year back. Orangeview had been so generous to me that I felt some guilt about leaving. I would always be grateful to them, but the move seemed strategic. The lure was a principal for whom I had great respect, the opportunity to teach a class of mentally gifted minors, and a school closer to my condo.

I made the decision before it dawned on me that I would have to do a second School Reentry Program for myself and start all over with the explanations of what happened to me. Fortunately, my former colleague and roommate, Lynda, had become one of their guidance counselors, and she helped to prepare the way for me before I even showed up. I used the same format to educate both faculty and students, and once again, the reentry program became my ticket to freedom. It took all the fear and mystique away. I easily settled in and felt accepted in record time. The English department was a cohesive group, and I had the privilege of teaching alongside some innovative and dynamic teachers.

Several months passed by before my next recovery milestone approached.

The time came when I no longer needed my pressure garments. After a year or so, skin grafts mature and no longer need constant pressure to keep them flat and smooth. Because I had additional surgeries, I ended up wearing the mask longer as each new graft benefited from the pressure. It took two years before I was finally given the go-ahead from Dr. Furnas to take off the mask. With the thought of the new me soon to be on display for the world to see, the reality unnerved me. I was not comfortable yet in my new skin. The mask had become a safe place, and people were accustomed to me wearing it. My body had changed, and with change came the anxiety of acceptance. I pondered the question, how could I navigate the public with fewer intrusive stares? I simply wanted to live my life and blend in to society without being constantly on my guard for the next comment someone made or the lingering looks. Regarding my job at school, I wasn't so much worried about fellow colleagues as I was the frankness of my junior high students who wouldn't pull punches in their reactions to me. And this new reveal seemed more personal than them accepting the mask.

It would be unbearable to hear one of them say, "Wow! I thought you would look a lot better. Is that really all they can do?"

I wondered if cosmetics could play a role in my post-mask reentry. Plenty of women without a burn injury applied makeup before they left their homes every day. They probably took for granted the blessing of a symmetrical lip line, even skin tone, and natural eyebrows that all worked together to create harmony in their faces. I longed for all three.

My relationship with cosmetics before my accident had been minimal, though positive. I wore a light foundation, some mascara, and eye shadow. I now needed the maximum. Looking in the mirror, I was at a loss about where to begin on my own. Once again, I looked to Hollywood with its plethora of beauty-based services and salons to tap into.

My friend Suzye offered to help me find just the right makeup artist. The consummate organizer and researcher of all my friends who have supported me, she could be trusted the most to find the best option. One day in early March, she sat down with the phone book and started dialing.

"Hi, I'm calling to see if your salon works with burn victims," Suzye said.

"Bird victims? No, what are you talking about?"

"No, b-u-r-n victims. You know, for someone who has been in a fire."

"Umm, no, we don't have any experience with people like that. Perhaps another salon…"

After two hours of calling, Suzye found only two salons willing to work with me. The lack of response shocked us both. Why were there so few resources for someone who needed help with their appearance more than most? Why didn't the burn center or my burn surgeon refer me to someone with this specialty? With new patients discharging every week with facial scars, how did they not even think about our challenges? With five burn centers in southern California, I realized the number of people needing image enhancement was not small. It was a puzzle I would spend many years trying to solve.

Of the two options, I chose Aida Grey. She was a woman with a world-renowned reputation and a very upscale salon in the center of Beverly Hills.

Judy and I hopped on the 405 Freeway north from Seal Beach and dodged traffic on a weekday morning in late March. We segued over to the Santa Monica Freeway and exited on Wilshire Boulevard an hour later. After finding a parking spot in a metered lot, we were in awe and felt dwarfed as we approached the fourteen-foot magnificently carved silver doors of Aida's salon, showcasing beauty wonderland. We walked in to see chic, well-dressed women with perfect skin and exquisitely coiffed hair waiting for services. If my body image had ever felt inadequate, it was at its peak in this environment. Half-expecting the receptionist to tell me I must have the wrong establishment, I was surprised when she smiled and said, "Aida will be right with you. Please have a seat."

We didn't have to wait long. A small-statured slightly plump woman in her sixties approached us. She had the most flawless, porcelain-like skin I had ever seen. Aida introduced herself and walked us past all the perfect ladies to a private room at the side of the salon.

I appreciated her sensitivity. I would have felt on display out there among the beauties. I sensed warmth and empathy emanating from Aida. She didn't ask what happened to soothe her curiosity. Instead, she jumped into action. It was as if she understood at some deep level that my expectations didn't border on the miraculous. I was a woman just trying to get a semblance of a normal face back.

I peeled off my wig and chin strap mask to begin.

She studied the reveal for long moments. "Barbara, I want to help you. I think some of my products will be really beneficial. I am going to mix up a custom base color that will harmonize the various skin tones of your face to give you one skin tone color. Then we will move on to creating a natural, more symmetrical lip line and eyebrows."

At her words, my heart leapt with pure joy that she might be able to give me an image that fostered normalcy and confidence in public settings. I desperately wanted to blend into a crowd and not have my scars be the focus.

After comparing several shades against my forehead and cheeks, she concocted a midrange color to use. Her canvas had a patchwork quilt to contend with, red scar lines swirling here and there across my left cheek. My grafted forehead had a much whiter appearance than the lower half of my face. The reconstructed tip of my nose was red and blotchy. Some of the lower cheek areas were a motley pinkish color down the length of my neck below my chin.

Aida patted the base color along the scar lines for a uniform coverage, working her way from section to section, smoothing the discoloration away.

"Barbara, notice how I am patting with the sponge from area to area with gentle lifts to give the maximum effect. You don't want to swipe across the skin, or you will make the coverage too light."

When satisfied the smoothness and color had been evenly gained, Aida applied a translucent powder to seal the effect. For my eyebrows, she used a medium brown pencil, placing small dots to create an arch above my eye, feathering in the color with swift strokes to complete the line.

"Eyebrows are delicate and difficult. You will have to practice to get this right. But they are very important because they frame your entire face and create expression."

My asymmetrical lips came next. My lower lip had retained a uniform fullness, but the upper lip had a straight scar line running the width of it without a cupid's bow. With a lip pencil, she drew the bow, forming the upper lip to look more natural. She filled in the lines with a soft shade of pink. She also applied a bit of mascara and a light neutral eye shadow to accent the color of my blue eyes.

After two hours of detailed work and instruction, my face had been transformed. Gone were the ragged lines and uneven tones, leaving a more normal face in view. I could hardly believe such a difference could be achieved. It gave me hope for the possibilities, though I was worried I hadn't truly learned yet to repeat her skilled work.

She didn't let me leave without a supply of makeup, the tools I would need, and a step-by-step sheet of instructions. As she did for all her clients, the custom blend for my base color was kept on file for future needs. She had built her reputation on individual service rather than mass production. I appreciated the personal touch.

As we were leaving, I walked back through the flawless crowd with far less awkwardness. I wanted to give Aida an exuberant hug but restrained myself. I warmly thanked her, holding back tears with difficulty. Her compassion was a gift this day.

Judy and I decided to treat ourselves before leaving Beverly Hills and went to the Bistro Garden for lunch. It seemed a good day to celebrate. It also became a test for my new look.

We walked in and were seated almost immediately in the outdoor area. The waiter approached our table and greeted me first, not averting his eyes and talking only to Judy, as had happened at past outings. After he took our order, I discreetly glanced around and didn't notice other diners staring and whispering. It felt good. Extremely good.

I plotted and planned for the perfect day to go to school without the garments. I strategized that a Thursday made the most sense for this new reentry. If my junior high students reacted negatively, it would be close to the weekend when I could spend lots of time on extra practice with the makeup. My first attempts had been a bit of a disaster. What had taken Aida a short amount of time took me triple. The fine motor skills required to pat, powder, and apply the more dense makeup challenged my hands greatly. The first time I tried to do my eyebrows, I threw the pencil across the bathroom in frustration and cried. I knew I needed several weeks more to practice before I set the date.

Thursday, April 26, 1979

I got up early and removed my mask for the last time. I thought about burning it in a small ceremony, but then considered the notion to be a little too dramatic. Instead, I folded it gently and set it in the drawer next to my prosthetic hands. Both items represented milestones in my journey I needed to hold on to for a little longer.

It was time to get ready. As part of the long-anticipated plan, I put on my favorite blue shirtwaist dress with a rich navy leather belt and reached for my makeup basket.

An hour later, I was satisfied with the result in the mirror and headed to Pine Junior High. My heart pounded and my stomach knotted up as I parked the car and made my way into the school. Today's test with the new me no longer hidden would forever be a milestone in my psyche.

The first person to see me as I walked through the front doors was the maintenance man, Harry. Harry was a short, balding, bespectacled man who was loved by the kids because he always had a joke and a smile for them. He tipped his chin and gave me his famous grin.

"Good morning, Barbara. You are lookin' good!"

I thanked him and continued to the main office to check my mailbox. The teachers' lounge was my next destination for one more needed cup of coffee. Several of the usual early birds were there, my new teaching partner Joyce among them.

She double-glanced at me and smiled. "Barbara, you are not wearing your mask. The makeup looks fantastic. How did you learn to do that? Your face looks really smooth."

I shared briefly about Aida Gray and the practice attempts over a two-month period. The entire group seemed impressed with my process and fortitude.

I finally made my way to my classroom. One of my ninth graders was standing by her locker and caught my eye as I drew near. Her eyes widened, and she turned fully toward me.

"Wow, Miss K., it must feel so good to be out of that mask. You look great!"

I held back tears as I responded to her kind words, the relief palpable as my breathing slowed and anxiety lessened. Junior high students didn't deserve their bad reputation on a day like today.

About to enter my room, an eighth grade boy caught my attention.

"Miss K. Cool. Does this mean you don't have to wear that mask anymore?"

"No. And I am so glad I don't ever have to wear it again," I said with a grin.

To a student, everyone in each of my six classes had only kind words and smiles to bestow on me, at least to my face, and their good will set the tone for this difficult transition back to a new life.

Over the next year, I kept adjusting to the new me, trying to form a new identity after the fire. When I had time off school, Dr. Furnas made a few modifications with surgeries to help my mouth look straighter and my nose better shaped. I was reaching deep to discover who I truly was on the inside. It was a battle. My days at school were filled with activity and meaning. But then the weekend hit, and I had moments of feeling lost and alone, the grief welling up and pressing in on me. My accident had opened a new world to me, good and bad. Painful memories clung, and I had to decide where I went from here. I wanted my suffering to count for something. I had a desperate desire that it all not be in vain. Could any good come from such devastation?

About a year after my injury, my occupational therapist Shirley and I had spearheaded the burn survivor support group I regularly attended. On the first Monday of every month, we invited former patients and their loved ones to sit down together, to listen and learn from each other. We talked about the challenges currently being faced and answered questions from new survivors. Would they be able to go back to work and perform the same job? How long would a company hold a place for them with months of rehab? How could they find new training if going back wasn't possible? Going on disability was frowned upon, but what were the other options? Sharing with each other became an empowering element of recovery. We didn't want anyone to feel like they were all alone in their struggles.

During our meetings in the burn center conference room, I got to know kids who were thrown back into the school system after a burn injury with no support. One example was Michele, a seventh grade girl with a shy and sweet disposition. Her burn injury occurred when her pajama top caught on fire from a lit candle in her bedroom. The flames damaged part of her neck, left cheek, and lips, requiring grafts. The skin remained slightly puckered and the lip line crooked, the scars obvious to her junior high schoolmates.

She described to our support group some of the treatment she received.

"It started the first week I went back. Stupid boys came up to me and made pig noises, whispering 'snout face' when I turned to glare at them. I have become their favorite target, and no one stands up for me. I have complained to several teachers, but it only makes the wretched boys more sneaky. When I walk by, they tap their lips and laugh. I hate them. Sometimes, I don't go to school. I hate my life."

The story of bullying made us grit our teeth and fish for something to say to encourage Michele.

"If you were my daughter, I would go to that school and kick their sorry asses, pardon my French," said a burly sixty-something gentleman.

"I wish I had a dad to do exactly that, but my father bailed on my mom and me years ago, so it's just us," said Michele.

"You are braver than you realize, Michele. I, for one, am proud of you for hanging in there this far," said a college-aged gal with hidden scars.

I had to say something.

"You know, Michele, I was a lot older than you when I was burned, but I relied on the buddy system constantly those first few years. I never wanted to go anywhere without a friend. Try to arrange to have one of your girlfriends with you all the time to give you confidence. They can stick up for you and maybe shame those awful boys into behaving better."

Although we came up with some empathizing statements, the conversation left me sitting there internally frustrated and fuming.

If only…if only we could have eased her way from day one. Maybe there would always be a bully or two waiting in the wings, but an early intervention could have rallied support from the majority of the kids. She shouldn't have to feel so alone and unsupported. No child should hate the thought of going to school. Or of living life.

Driving home from the support group after hearing Michele's story, thoughts of my father came to mind. I wondered about the difference he could have made in my own recovery if he had been alive and present through the dark times. I had a few precious memories of him that I clung to. They have only become more poignant over the years since my childhood on our farm in Iowa.

My witty dad.

My kind dad.

My hardworking dad.

He had been of average height and lean from farm chores. His rugged face bore beautiful hazel-gray eyes and a cleft chin that fascinated me as a little girl. I had one like his, though less pronounced. Premature gray hair and slight balding complemented his farmer tan most of the year. I loved the twinkle in his eye and the personal nicknames he made up for those closest to him.

His strong hands held my world together. Dancing with my mother and me to a lively tune on the *Ed Sullivan Show*, flashing black-and-white in our front parlor. Cradling a sleeping me out of his big chair and carrying his cherished bundle up to the bedroom to tuck me in, whispering, "Sweet dreams, punkins."

I could go toe-to-toe with my mother to get my way, but I so doted on my dad that I never wanted to risk disappointing him. I never regretted the mischief I gave up to garner his approval. His existence gave me great security.

I loved taking care of the animals with my father, following in his footsteps doing chores. In his shadow, I learned lessons of life. He taught me to labor with my heart, relish a sunrise, plow a straight path with my intentions. I knelt by his side to watch the tiny calves being born, slick with the promise of new breath, taking tentative but faltering steps. The responsibility to care for the little ones fell on our shoulders.

"Until they can stand on their own, punkins, we have to watch out for them."

And we did. Simple things consistently given. Food and water. Protection. Even one day could not be missed. To be a farmer required 100 percent commitment.

My father's example prepared me to be a teacher, a wonderful job that benefited the next generation. But more than ever, I was concerned about the strugglers, the bullied, the kids trying to rebuild their lives after a trauma. For better or worse, my life was invested in recovery. I had some experience to share.

Disabled children had a rough time in the school systems of the years prior to the American Disabilities Act of 1984. Many parents kept them home for protection rather than exposing them to ridicule and misunderstanding. As a teacher, I believed that it was a kid's job to return to school after an injury, just like it was an adult's job to return to work. It provided the best long-term outcomes for community reentry. Schools became complicit in marginalizing kids. It may not have been intentional, but the end result left disabled children treated as outcasts. I learned that many burn-injured children were recommended for special education classes, even though they had no learning problems. Administrators feared that kids with visible scars would be a disturbance to kids without an injury. Therefore, many kids were encouraged to be homeschooled, thinking it would be easier for the child in the long run. However, keeping children isolated from their peers and school life made them feel isolated and unworthy, causing more harm to them personally in their recovery and academically.

I felt in my heart that I had to watch out for the survivor children from the burn center, for those taking faltering steps. Until they could stand on their own. Still taking tentative steps toward my own recovery, I wasn't sure how much I could give. But I could try. Maybe we could help each other.

8

The Leap

For three years, starting in the fall of 1977, Dr. Furnas slowly put my face back together, one procedure at a time. We were a team. But the day came when I needed to graduate from surgery. It was time to let go of any lingering false hope that he could restore me perfectly. I had learned the hard truth that disfigurement is only diminished by surgical intervention, not overcome.

We met in his office and reminisced. The walls displayed photographs from frequent trips to Kenya he had taken with his wife, Mary Lou, and their work with the East Africa Flying Doctors Service. Wooden carvings created by African artists covered the shelves of a bookcase in the corner. Organized stacks of medical books and patient files filled the desktop. They reminded me of his influence spread far beyond this small corner of the world.

I looked at Dr. Furnas's hands resting on the mahogany desk. Because of my own loss, I continued to notice people's hands in a whole new way. His were medium-sized with long, tapered fingers, graceful and perfectly proportioned for the delicate work of a skilled reconstructive surgeon. But the truly beautiful thing about them was how much they had shaped this new life of mine. What words could I find to express my appreciation for the meticulous care he had shown me? I floundered.

"Dr. Furnas, I don't know how to thank you for all you've done. It's not possible. I wouldn't even know where to begin…" I shook my head, willing myself not to cry.

He gave me that gentle smile of his, the kind eyes seeing past my stumbling words.

"Barbara, I can truly say it has been a remarkable journey with you. My patients have been the most profound professors in my career. And you are one of them. You came in so persistent and determined, wanting your former appearance back. I wish that had been possible. And yet, I knew that with time, you would have the strength to handle the transition to whatever it would be."

I remembered the numerous questions I asked him when we first started working on the reconstructive surgeries.

"I kept asking you in what I thought were subtly creative ways to get the answer I wanted to hear. Thanks for being so patient with me when I asked fifteen times in fifteen different ways if you could make me look like I did before," I said with a laugh.

"I wish there was more that I could do, but for now, time is on your side. The redness will continue to fade. The scars will likely soften up more as the years go by. From a surgeon's viewpoint, with the extent of your burn, your appearance is quite an improvement— and attractive, if I do say so myself."

His smile widened, the ruefulness apparent.

I smiled back and asked a final question I hoped wouldn't annoy him.

"I want to keep in contact with you. Would that be okay…if I dropped in on you from time to time?"

A quick nod. "Of course. You always know where to find me."

He rose from his chair to escort me, a giant presence at my side, lending courage to take this exodus out of his office. Out of his care. But not out of his heart.

I turned and hugged him fiercely.

And walked through the door into the next chapter of my life.

Now that I had completed my reconstructive surgeries, other endeavors that had been germinating came to the surface. I kept thinking about Michele and the bullies at her school. I decided to work on designing a reentry program specific to the survivor children and young adults I ran into like her at our support group.

I was on a quest. Surely some programs already existed that I could learn from as I planned one my burn center could use. This was 1980. We had come far in our health-care system. Several thousand people were burned every year. There must be some organizations with resources.

I posed the question to my friend, Andrew McGuire. Andrew was a burn survivor who I met at our support group when he came as a speaker. He had hidden burns from a childhood injury. His pajamas caught a spark from the family fireplace when he was seven years old. As an adult, with his Kevin Costner good looks and wonderful smile, he encouraged people with possibilities beyond their imagination. He became the director of a burn foundation in San Francisco and advocated for flame-retardant children's clothing and had recently taken up the fight for a fire-safe cigarette. I was in awe of him. Taking on the tobacco companies couldn't be an easy endeavor.

Andrew recommended that I turn to the American Burn Association (ABA) for ideas for my school reentry program. This professional medical organization was founded in 1967 and was committed to improving care to patients via education, research, and fostering prevention.

Attending my first ABA meeting in Washington, DC, in 1982 opened my eyes to reality. While medical breakthroughs to treat burns continued to increase, programs and interventions for survivors were practically nonexistent. In my search, I found one school reentry program at the Shriners Children's Hospital in Boston.

One.

And in my eyes, it lacked completeness, with a focus on orienting students in only one or two classrooms. Burn-injured children garnered the attention of the whole school. My school reentry plan involved educating the entire student body about a returning child or teenager. The biggest problems could arise in the hallways between classes, on the playground, or in the cafeteria where everyone hung out. I believed the presentation should happen in several school assemblies, gathering a few grades at a time.

A personalized slideshow would portray the journey the survivor has experienced. It would start with the interior of a burn center and some of the equipment used in the healing process. Pictures of the child working with a physical therapist and some of the progress at each stage of recovery. I would visit the home and take more photos of the child in his or her pressure garments surrounded by siblings, pets, and other family members. The pictures would help to show the courage of the child who endured burn care and multiple procedures, fostering an understanding of the returning student. Most importantly, the presentation would convey that the student remained the same person post-injury, even though his or her skin may look different. It also would provide helpful instruction for fellow students on how to act and what to say. And what *not* to say. Bombarding returning kids with a litany of questions can overwhelm rather than show concern.

A buddy system needed to be put in place the first few weeks back at school, making sure the survivor had someone to eat lunch and hang out with during free time. The special attention and training could make all the difference. The program would also model how to handle stares, questions, and teasing for the survivor and the parents.

After formulating my plan, I made an appointment with Susan, the social worker at UC Irvine. She loved my ideas. Part of me wanted to hand them off and let someone at the burn center run with them. I was not looking for a huge project. My day job kept me busy and fully occupied. I broached the subject.

"Susan, will this program be useful to you?"

"Useful? Yes. Realistic? No. I'm working overtime to handle our inpatient load. I don't have the hours for aftercare. Our patients are complicated. Some days I can barely come up with a discharge plan for them. Follow up? I just don't have the time."

"Would the burn center hire someone for this?"

She laughed at my naivety. "Have you heard the phrase 'Treat 'em and street 'em'? Don't get me wrong. I love our staff. We have phenomenal surgeons, nurses, and therapists who care. But as soon as they save a life, they consider their job done. It's the medical culture."

"Is it really that big a leap? To think about the social challenges a person with visible burns faces out in their communities—the stares, the questions, the double takes when they leave the burn center?" I asked.

"They may think about it, but to do something? The surgeons especially have incredibly busy, stressful schedules. It's a dilemma, Barbara. I don't have any answers for you."

I turned again to my friend Andrew McGuire for some more advice. With his typical brisk pace, he walked into the coffee shop where we agreed to meet. A visionary to the core, Andrew seemed to be the perfect person who I could trust with my dilemma. His advice surprised me.

"*You* have to make them care, Barbara. Why don't you apply for a grant and run the reentry program yourself? You are a teacher who is also a survivor. It's a great combo. The money's out there. You just have to go after it," he said.

"Me? Schools will freak out when they see me coming. My junior high has gotten used to me, but I think they are an exception. To walk into a bunch of new schools seems very risky."

"Not if you have the backing of the burn centers. If they buy into your program and give you referrals, you have an instant in! You need to model this—be an advocate for all survivor students. You understand how schools work. You know how to put an effective presentation together and deliver it to students. Who is more qualified than you?" he asked.

Who was more qualified than I? I wanted to say, "Anyone and everyone." But I knew Andrew had a point. But to go from classroom teacher to survivor advocate seemed daunting, risky, a vault into unknown territory. Yet these were two familiar worlds in my life colliding. Who's to say they wouldn't meld? Having the courage to try remained the bigger obstacle.

One year. I could give it a year and see what would happen.

I decided to apply for a leave of absence from my teaching position for the 1983–1984 academic year and submitted a grant proposal to the Weingart Foundation in Los Angeles. I kept it simple, sharing my journey and the basics of a reentry program. I had heard about this particular foundation from the parents of one of my students, whose uncle sat on the board of directors. They specialized in providing funds for health, human services, and education, especially to the disadvantaged. I was hoping the connection might work in my favor.

A letter with the organization's logo arrived two months later. I opened the mailbox, and my heartbeat spiked at the sight of the envelope sitting on top of the small pile. Picking it up and ripping the seal, I paused and sensed the weight of this pivotal moment. This lapsed Catholic had even marshaled up a few prayers over it. I began to read.

Dear Miss Kammerer,

We are pleased to inform you that your grant request has been accepted…

The elation welled up, and tears followed. The validation sunk in. A group of individuals had deemed my project worthwhile, seen that it could impact struggling children. I was honored to be chosen, anxious to get started.

Using contacts from my own burn center, University of California Irvine, I wanted to offer my program to all of southern California. A local burn foundation had graciously allowed me to channel the Weingart funds through their organization. The connection gave me further legitimacy in the region.

The vetting process began in the fall of 1983. The first meeting took place at the Los Angeles County-USC Burn Center, with staff attending from the rehabilitation institute associated with them, Rancho Los Amigos Medical Center. I rolled in my slide projector on its makeshift metal cart and set up for a presentation to about twenty-five medical professionals in a small conference room at the burn center. I pulled out my slide tray and clicked it into the projector slot on top, hoping none of my slides were upside down or out of order.

Two imposing figures led the group. Dr. Bruce Zawacki, chief of the burn center, and Dr. Garry Brody, chief of plastic surgery and burn rehabilitation at Rancho Los Amigos. They were both well-respected players in the burn world of California and of the nation.

Dr. Zawacki, tall, lanky, and handsome, with silver hair and blue eyes, introduced me with little fanfare.

"This is Barbara Kammerer. She is a burn survivor who was treated at UC Irvine. She works as a junior high teacher and has developed a program for kids to help them return to school more easily. Please welcome her."

I started by sharing a bit of my story and showed them what a basic presentation would look like. An important aspect of my program was the individualization of each child's story, with a home visit to meet the family to understand the child's needs. I shared photographs of the survivor playing games and interacting with parents, siblings, and pets to give a feel of the home environment.

My nerves partially settled as I got into my explanation. At the end, I didn't sense a lot of reaction from the group, making me wonder if any interest had been generated.

Dr. Zawacki asked the first question. "How long do you wait between giving the reentry presentation and sending the child back to the school environment?"

"The next day or within the next week," I answered.

"Okay, that makes sense. But how quickly should a child be expected to return to school after a severe injury?"

"I think it should be as soon as the burn center staff deem the child's skin has healed enough and is able to tolerate the pressure garments."

"Wouldn't it be less stressful on the child to be homeschooled for the first year post-injury? To be in a more protected environment?" asked one of the occupational therapists.

"Just like it's important for an adult to go back to work, we need to think of school as a child's work. The healthiest option is for the child to go back into the environment he or she was used to—a place where the child can succeed and thrive again, rather than be isolated and kept from learning to deal with the world. Children need to have a chance to be around their peers, to play and explore with others."

The doctors looked at each other and raised their eyebrows. Dr. Brody, a portly bald man in his midfifties, turned to me, pursed his lips, and asked another question.

Sensing this one would be important, I braced myself for possible rejection.

"How do you suggest that we make referrals to you?"

I sighed in relief. They saw the value.

* * *

The grant opened a whole new realm of teaching possibilities. Student by student, I began to help kids and adults adjust to being back in the public eye. The first kids I worked with were the Hererra boys. Omar, a six-year-old, and Fabian, nine, were burned playing with matches in their front yard while their mother, Roxanna, was lying down with a headache in the house. Fabian required skin grafts on his face and hands. Omar's scars were more hidden, with grafts to his torso and legs. They attended a small Catholic school in Downey where everyone knew about the fire and their hospitalization. Roxanna worried how the other kids would treat her boys. She was a wise mother and instinctively knew that the longer she waited to put them back in school, the harder it would be.

With two children recovering from burns, she had her hands full: dressing changes, bathing rituals, med regiments, pressure garments, physical therapy, doctor's appointments. The cry of her heart was for them to be normal boys again, playing, laughing, and fitting in. I hoped I could help make that happen.

Roxanna and I walked into the office at Our Lady of Perpetual Help Elementary School the day of the reentry program. A wary silence greeted us as I asked to speak to the principal, Mr. Jones. He came out of his office looking nervous, his eyes darting back and forth between Roxanna and me. He escorted us to the first presentation, held in a small multipurpose room. The first group we met with were the kindergarteners and first graders. They sat on the carpeting in rows, legs crossed, waiting patiently with their hands in their laps. About seventy-five children stared up at me with eager little faces.

Mr. Jones introduced me with a stern voice. "Kids, we have Ms. Kammerer here today to talk to you. Most of you know the Herrera boys, who have been in the hospital for burn treatment, but will be coming back to school this week. Now pay attention to the important information she has to share, and remember your best manners."

I could guess his thoughts, his worry that the kids would say something disrespectful to me or react in some manner that would embarrass the school. As a junior high teacher, the prospect didn't faze me. I took command of the assembly.

"Good morning! I'm here to speak to you about Omar and Fabian, who have had a burn injury. I'm going to give you more detail about their injuries and recovery, but first, I'm sure you have some curiosity about me and my burn injury, so let me tell you a bit about my story."

I shared about my accident, the valiant rescue by a Good Samaritan, and being rushed with sirens blaring to the burn center.

"I spent several months there. Does anyone know what a burn center is? Let me show you some pictures. Just like me, Fabian and Omar had to be at this special place for many weeks."

I began the slide presentation with an image of the two boys at the hospital. I explained what happened to them and how brave they had been to go through such painful treatment. I passed around a set of the pressure garments as an example of what the boys now wore. It gave the kids a chance to see and feel what they were like, and I followed up the show-and-tell with an explanation of why the pressure was needed.

Their little hands grasped the stiff tan fabric as they passed it from one student to the next. One boy with freckles and a mischievous smile pulled it as hard as he could to see if it would tear.

I smiled at his antics and continued. "Another benefit of the pressure garments is to enable the boys to do all of the activities they did before. They will want to ride their bikes and play sports. The garments will protect their new skin from the sun for that first year, along with a hat. They will also be able to help around the house and, of course, clean up their rooms," I said.

I ignored the shaking heads about the cleaning comment and kept going.

"I lost the fingers of my right hand in the accident, and although my hands are not perfect, look what I can do."

I picked up a piece of chalk within the grip area of my little hand and wrote my name on the board. Their eyes got bigger, and several gasped. I shook hands with a teacher and pretended that I was driving a car. The little ones started to grin, seeing my hand in a whole new light.

Sensing the questions brimming in their eyes, I invited the kids to voice them.

"Can you make mac and cheese?" a gal with pigtails asked.

"That one's easy," I said.

"What about a hamburger?" another chimed in.

"Yes. I have lots of kitchen gadgets that help me cook and clean and do all sorts of things, even gardening."

"Could you feed my Cabbage Patch doll?" a boisterous little redhead said from the front row.

"I think I could manage that too," I said, trying not to laugh.

The unease dissipated quickly. Wariness turned to warmth as the kids were carried along on the journey—mine, Fabian's, and Omar's. The pictures said a thousand words. My explanations fostered an atmosphere of curiosity being satisfied.

At the end, the principal closed our time together, and his demeanor had changed. His words were effusive with praise and encouragement.

"Now I want you to thank Ms. Kammerer, kids."

Their heads all bobbed, and they eagerly replied, "Thank you, Ms. Kammerer."

We repeated our program to the second and third graders next, followed by the fourth and fifth graders, and then the sixth grade by themselves. Around six hundred kids heard our presentation that day. As the principal's comfort level increased, Mr. Jones's introduction got longer and more effusive. He clearly recognized the importance of a school reentry program.

We all left on a high note.

Walking out to our cars, Roxanna and I took a few moments to discuss how the presentations went. Her thoughts bounced from one to the next, but her summary gave me pause.

"Barbara, the school's relationship with you went from wary to wonderful in about five seconds. I don't know how you did it, but they were captivated from the get-go. You walked in as a somewhat suspicious scarred person, and walked out a hero."

"Well, I think *hero* is a little strong, but I have learned that people just need real interaction—to see a glimpse beyond the scars," I responded. "We fear someone who looks different, or talks different, or acts different. If you can help someone get past their initial fears or discomfort, it helps in a big way."

As I drove home from Downey, exhausted but thrilled, I ruminated on the importance of the school reentry program for Omar and Fabian. I had one chance with these kids who were their peers, just a few hours, to make a difference for the boys. It reminded me that the presentations had to be as effective as I could make them.

Thinking about the principal's first reaction to me, wary and somewhat negative, I had a fear that school personnel would balk at letting me speak to their students. My strategy became not disclosing to them that I was a burn survivor myself before the day I walked into the schools. The surprise could turn out to be a bit awkward for me, but I was willing to handle that as long as nothing would stop me from reaching my goal of paving the way.

A week later, I checked in with Roxanna tee how Omar and Fabian were doing. A cheery tone resonated in her voice as she explained how good the boys seemed to be coping. They had not been bullied or shunned playing outside at recess. Their classmates felt free to ask questions and interact.

"Barbara, I know your program has made the difference. I'm sure it won't all be smooth sailing, but we are taking one day at a time. Thank you so much for helping my boys."

My satisfaction from hearing these sweet words was immense. It helped relieve any doubts about the vital role a school reentry program could play in the lives of young survivors. It gave meaning to my own journey. One school at a time, I could hopefully make a difference in the lives of survivors, families, and a whole student body.

But even if these two precious boys were the only ones I would be able to help, I knew that I had not leapt in vain.

9

―――――

Battles

I had to stop calling myself a lapsed Catholic. The truth was far more complex. They say there are no atheists in a war bunker. I could list the big spiritual battles of my life: my father's death when I was twelve, the divorce from my Catholic husband when I was twenty-seven, my car crash at age thirty-three.

As an only child, I loved church. In small agricultural communities, churches provided not only spiritual connection, but also social activities and a sense of belonging. To be part of a big family comforted me. It gave me some semblance of brothers and sisters, aunts and uncles, grandmothers and grandfathers. I felt safe surrounded by a community of people who cared about me. I belonged.

Along the way, my faith got battered by time and trials, disillusionment and discontentment. Like many of my age group who were influenced by secular culture, I wandered. I rationalized not going to Mass. The majority of my friends did not attend church, and none of the men I dated did. My faith seemed to slip away one Sunday at a time. What had following the rules given me besides the harsh stigma of being divorced? I looked for an excuse to avoid facing that shame.

After the fire, I relied on the faith of others to see me through. A group of Catholic ladies called the Blue Angels prayed consistently for me over the course of my hospital stay and subsequent surgeries. My mother and my aunt Gen, a former nun working as a teacher for most of her career, also prayed diligently. I had examples of faith around me. A longtime friend, Claire, wandered like me, but was eventually lured back to faith. I watched and listened, curious about the changes in her life. She had a serenity that I longed for.

Part of my recovery involved seeking the meaning of things for myself. The grant had given me new purpose for my career. But I was lonely. With no significant other or siblings, my plethora of close friends were my only family besides my mother and aunt.

At age thirty-nine, I got a phone call from my aunt Gen back in Iowa. Usually a bright and cheery soul, the lack of levity in her tone clued me in that something serious was on the horizon, a new wave about to crash into my life.

"Barbara, your mother hasn't been feeling well for a while, and we went in for some testing…It's ovarian cancer. I think she suspects something serious, but we haven't told her yet. I wanted to call you first."

I sat down quickly in the nearest chair, stunned and shaking. "Aunt Gen, are they sure it's cancer? I can't believe this. I need to talk to the doctor, and I want to be there when she's told…Wait for me. I will get the next flight that I can."

I hung up the phone and paced the living room of my condo, feeling sick. Sobs rumbled up through my chest. All I could think about was losing her, and the very idea spun me into a panic. I tried to catch my breath, doubling over gulping in air. When I had a semblance of breath back, I grabbed the phone to call Judy. Several rings passed before I heard her voice.

"Judy, my mother…" I choked off the sentence and tried to find my voice again.

"Oh my, what's wrong? What's happened, Barbara? You sound scared."

"My mother…She has cancer—ovarian."

"Oh no. I'm so sorry. I can be with you in an hour. Hold on…"

I hung up the phone, relieved she could be with me. I needed to call an agency to buy a plane ticket to Iowa, pack, make arrangements to get to the airport. The details piled up in my head, but inertia kept me from acting on anything. Instead, I sat on my living room sofa in a daze. I couldn't escape the racing thoughts. Vivid memories of my father surfaced.

* * *

Standing by the water fountain in the hallway outside my seventh-grade classroom, I loitered a bit before returning to class after lunch. Several of my classmates were milling about as well. No need to rush back to a math class, right? We took turns taking drinks at the fountain, teasing one another and goofing off. School usually made me happy. I could let the social part of me shine amid homework drudgeries. As a beloved only daughter, safety and security surrounded me on a daily basis. It gave me confidence.

Turning around, I was surprised to see my neighbor, Vernie Carter, purposefully heading up the stairs toward me. His sober gaze locked onto mine. Dressed in his usual farm clothes, blue-striped bib overalls, and a chambray work shirt, the strained look on his face scared me. As soon as I heard the words "I have some bad news," I somehow intuitively knew what was coming.

And I wailed, the sounds of my cries echoing shrilly through the school, piercing the ears of every student.

"Daddy…Oh my daddy. No! No! No!"

My best friend, Pattie, ran to me and grabbed my arm. "Barbara, what's wrong? What happened?"

"My daddy is dead."

The stark words fell on a shocked crowd of students. My teacher, Mrs. Hadley, sent the kids to the classroom and ushered me to the nearby wall where our coats hung in a long line.

Only part of me registered movement as I gathered my wool jacket and lunch pail, walking down the stairs, zombielike, and out the front doors to be driven home. It was a blustery, cold April day, and I shivered in his old truck. My numb mind fought to stay engaged.

When we arrived at the farm, I ran inside calling for my mother. Mrs. Carter greeted me from the parlor and told me she was in the guest room. I flew up the stairs and found her lying on the bed with her arms crossed tightly against her face. Her dark hair fanned out across the pillow, her normal demeanor frozen.

I curled up next to her on the bed, sobbing. She hugged me close and didn't speak for long moments.

"What happened?" I whispered.

She answered back with a sliver of a voice, "I was cleaning the kitchen, and I heard Duchess barking out front. I went to the window to see why she sounded so frantic, and I saw your father lying on the ground. I ran to him and dragged him all the way to the porch. He suffered a heart attack. I told him not to lift those big rocks by himself on the lower field. But you know your dad. He must have felt the pain and tried to get to me. I called Dr. Palmer, and he rushed here, but there was nothing he could do. Your dad was gone."

Her voice trailed off, and she tightened her grip on my arm. I pestered her with more questions, and she shook her head.

"No, sweetie, not now. I just need to lie here for a while longer by myself. You go down and ask Mrs. Carter to get you something to eat. And wait for your grandmother. Can you do that for me? She should be here soon with your aunts."

I made myself get up and go downstairs. I didn't feel like eating, so I went out to the porch to wait for Grandma Kammerer, feeling lost and wishing I could just hide away from everyone with my mother.

Instead, I became hostess with Mrs. Carter to greet friends and family rushing over to share in the grief. With time, I understood that my mother had suffered a great shock and had mentally curled in on herself. She had little emotional energy to give me that day. As the long day waned, I slipped away from everyone and clung to Duchess, our cocker spaniel, for comfort by the side of the house, away from prying eyes.

Reality hit after everyone left late that night. My father would never again walk into the mudroom after a long day of farm chores, cheerily asking about supper. His teasing, twinkling eyes would never again fill my heart with a sense of well-being. No more help with my math challenges. No more tagging after him when my homework was done. No more tucking me safely into bed.

My childhood was at an end, and with it, a feeling of security that the bad things would always be held at bay. I no longer felt safe in our little farmhouse. I locked the doors, checked on my mom, and tried to sleep...

* * *

On the flight to Iowa the following afternoon, I realized I was praying about my mother. Did I believe someone was truly listening? It mattered more than ever. I had been inching back toward faith in the past few months, hungry for my connection with God. I had slipped into spiritual apathy at the dissolution of my first marriage, disillusioned that the perfect Catholic man I thought I had wisely married wasn't. My farm girl existence had never been exposed to cheating husbands, and the shock of his betrayal paralyzed my faith.

Our divorce caused a rift in my soul. I felt worthless, guilty, ashamed. A disappointment to God. To everyone. I had quickly changed my name back to Kammerer and tried to pretend it didn't matter. I moved back into the dating scene and lived life how I pleased. The denial fostered my wandering. Murray's temporary love and then defection in the face of adversity only reinforced my negative perceptions of myself.

But I didn't want to stay lost. I had been checking out churches, trying to discern where God would want me to be. But after Aunt Gen's phone call, I had a new mission, and I desperately needed His help. I couldn't let my mother die. I didn't want to be an orphan.

Landing at the Quad Cities airport, I found Aunt Gen and my mother waiting for me when I exited the plane. We drove the thirty minutes to the hospital covering the uneasy silence with chitchat, avoiding any serious conversation. There would be plenty of time for that.

Upon arriving at our destination, we made our way to the bank of doctors' offices. Aunt Gen and I sat on each side of my mother in the oncologist's exam room, ready to offer support.

In a matter-of-fact voice, Dr. Keally got right to the point. "Mrs. Kammerer, I'm sorry to tell you that you have stage 4 ovarian cancer. At seventy-three years of age, it is pretty serious…life-threatening."

My mother took in the news with her typical Midwest stoicism, barely responding to the oncologist's announcement. Her response reflected the German tendency of pushing one's emotions to the background and holding them deeply inside, not to be shared with others. Her passivity only fueled my reactivity. I rushed to throw out questions about treatment and steps to rid her of this life-threatening crisis. Aunt Gen and I set up her first surgery as soon as possible, with chemotherapy treatments to follow. With frenetic energy, I researched the mindset and actions needed to survive cancer. I purchased meditation tapes, the latest food supplements and nutrition books, anything I could get my hands on to aid in the fight ahead of us.

Spending the summer of 1982 in Iowa, I saw my mother through the surgery and several courses of chemotherapy. Each one brought her nausea and weakness, the strong chemicals racing through her body to kill the out-of-control cells. To prevent hair loss, the oncology nurse gave my mother an ice cap for her head. A helmetlike cover sat on top of the ice, anchoring it in place. With my mother's small four-foot-eleven-inch frame, the visual effect brought some levity to our day.

"Well, Mother, I don't think a football career would be the best retirement plan for you. Though you do look kind of cute in the helmet…"

Aunt Gen made up a little song. "In your chemo bonnet—with the ice upon it—you will be the grandest lady in the hospital today."

Mother gently shook her head and smiled at our antics. I prayed the wretched cells would die.

Leaving her to rest, Aunt Gen and I walked out to the lobby for a break and a cup of coffee. Aunt Gen always drew attention with her bright clothing. After wearing black for most of her adult career as a Catholic nun, her retirement wardrobe was all pink, yellow, aqua, and coral. That day she looked like a daffodil with a yellow dress and complimentary shoes. The outfit went well with her strawberry-blonde hair that she refused to let turn gray. A pearl necklace and earrings finished the outfit off perfectly.

We settled into a row of scooped plastic chairs adjacent to the elevators. My feet barely touched the floor, so I leaned forward to get more comfortable.

I voiced the unthinkable. "Aunt Gen, if Mom dies, you are the only one I have left...Could this really be God's plan? First Dad. Now Mom? I know God's disappointed in me. I haven't been very faithful to Him. Is that why?"

She took my hand and leaned in. "You think this is God's punishment?"

I nodded my head.

Her frown deepened. "I don't believe God is out to punish us when tragedy occurs. We live in a world full of danger and risk. He isn't the author of pain, though many jump to blame Him when anything goes wrong. Oh, Barbara, I wish I could answer the whys-of-life questions, but I can't. Have you tried leaning on Him? I feel like you've been on the run for a very long time."

Her words gave me pause. I mulled them over, looking everywhere but into her eyes. I finally acknowledged the truth to someone beside myself.

"Yeah, you're right. I felt abandoned, so I chose to stop thinking about Him. Now I just feel lost."

"As strange as this may sound, it's a place to start, my dear. Just tell God those feelings as you pray. He knows they are there."

I took a deep breath and let it out. Simple words, but they made me feel like screaming. Instead I whispered, "I'll try, Aunt Gen. I'll try. But we have to save Mother. I can't bear losing her..."

Through the chemotherapy, my mother continued to look robust. I never saw tears. Her mode of coping had always involved going deep within herself, shucking off any pity or sympathy. At the end of the summer, I made plans to return to California. She seemed better, and I was convinced we were on the road to complete healing.

I lined up services and continued treatment for her before my departure. I didn't question my steely determination to combat the disease. A mother's love and presence couldn't be replaced. Though I had often stepped into the caretaker role in our relationship, she had always been 100 percent committed to me and supportive of my life choices. I never asked her what she wanted regarding the cancer. She was quiet and resigned to whatever fate awaited.

Not I. God and I had a pact. I vowed to renew my commitment to Him and to Catholicism. He had to do His part. My plan had to work.

Christmas found me back with my mother to share the holiday. The cancer had spread and my despair with it. I made arrangements for her to come and live with me in California. We tried to make the best of her good days with trips to Laguna Beach, Catalina Island, and Santa Barbara. Playing tourist medicated my sadness. Part of me knew I was in denial, but I refused to give up. I scheduled more chemotherapy and consulted new oncologists.

On our last excursion to Santa Barbara, my mother became so ill that I had to rush her back to the medical center, a three-hour drive, where she was admitted for observation. Every week showed her failing a bit more. I heard about an excellent doctor at St. Joseph's Hospital in Orange County and moved my mother there in early April of 1983. I brought her spring flowers and tried to cheer her with stories of the kids I continued to help with the school reentry program. Most nights I spent on a cot in her room, wanting to be near in the night if she needed me.

The hospital staff came to know me well. One of them, Chaplain Jane, came to be a frequent visitor and stalwart supporter. She had a striking presence at five-foot-four with brilliant blue eyes and wavy blonde hair. She radiated an inner peace I desperately needed. Her empathy was my undoing.

"Barbara, you need to accept the fact that your mother is dying, and then help her live until that moment—no gloom and doom.

Share your heart with her, celebrate Mother's Day, provide a sense of normalcy, and love her to the end."

Her words penetrated, and tears erupted. I was losing the battle to cling to my denial. The pain was raw. I shook my head. Finally resigned.

She gave me a gentle hug, letting me cry.

My mother received a lot of support from the same friends who so attentively took care of me after my injury. They helped me carry the weight of the impending loss.

One night, Claire came to visit and brought a teddy bear with her for my mother to cuddle with. Her reaction surprised us both.

"Oh, thank you, but I wanted a bunny."

And she burst into tears.

Claire and I looked at each other with wide eyes and in disbelief that my mother would voice such disapproval. It was so out of character.

A few days later, Claire came back with a small fluffy bunny, and Mother was all smiles, delighted by the floppy ears and puffy white tail.

Mother's Day steadily approached. I decided to celebrate a week early with balloons and flowers while Mother was still conscious. She needed to know how much I appreciated her.

I walked into her hospital room with my arms full of goodies and watched her eyes widen in delight. I ignored her wan cheeks and the weakness in her hug, focusing on her smile. Sitting next to her on the bed, I took her hand into mine. How to find the words?

"Mom, you sacrificed so much for me after Dad's death. You graciously let me go live my life without ever making me feel guilty or burdened. That was a gift. And I don't think as a self-centered young girl I ever realized that or thanked you for it."

She shook her head. "Barbara dear, that's what parents are supposed to do. You raise a child to leave home and live…"

"Yes, but I was your only child and all you had left…I love you, Mom. And I'm so thankful for you and all the ways you have shown your love for me…" I couldn't stop the tears.

She patted my hand, a loving smile on her face. And my resignation turned to a measure of peace.

* * *

Sleeping on the cot, I was with her in the early morning hours of actual Mother's Day. I awakened to two nurses at my mom's bedside checking her vital signs. One nurse solemnly looked over at me and said, "Barbara, your mother's blood pressure is very low, only 40 over 20. She is in the death process. Is there someone you would like me to call?"

At four thirty in the morning, my options were limited.

"Yes, can you call Chaplain Jane for me?" I asked.

I didn't want to go through these final hours alone.

Chaplain Jane arrived quickly, and we sat on either side of my mother's bed, each holding a hand as the morning dawned. We talked quietly and prayed for my mother, loving her in these last hours. She didn't respond to our voices, but briefly opened her eyes at one point. I didn't think she really saw me. Her labored breathing became more and more shallow and then suddenly stopped. The room became utterly silent.

I turned to Jane, whispering, "Is Mother gone?"

Jane nodded her head and quietly left to call the nurse.

I looked at my mother and thought how fitting it was to hold the hand of the woman who gave me life as she serenely surrendered her own. An honor.

The circle of life.

Jane arranged for the morning Mass at the hospital to be dedicated to my mother. I stayed in the small chapel afterward, thankful to picture my mother in heaven, whole and at peace. I was glad for her until I began thinking about me. My pact with God hadn't worked out the way I had anticipated. Or should I say demanded? I wrestled with that.

God, why did you take my father so young and leave my mother and me alone? How could you let me choose a husband who seemed like a great young man, but then turned into someone the opposite? And then the fire. Will I ever be loved? Or will I always be alone? I need you to help my unbelief...

Jane sat down next to me, interrupting the cry of my heart. "Are you okay?"

"No. But I will be. I just have to reconcile my will with God's."

"Oh, that little endeavor," she said, lifting both eyebrows. Taking my hand, she looked intently at me. "You can lean on Him, Barbara. Don't you understand yet that you are never truly alone?"

"All I know is that I love to question Him, but then when I look back, I start counting up these graces amidst the struggles, little and big, that He has brought into my life. I see Him at work. I get glimmers of His love. I sensed Him in the room with us. It was so peaceful—actually beautiful."

Jane squeezed my hand, nodding her agreement.

And I understood that God had won the battle for my heart.

10

Tools

Despite my heart change, the whys-of-life questions never completely let go, especially regarding my car crash. The struggle to accept this new me remained: the limited use of my hands, whether to tell the short story or the long version of my injury to people I met. The challenges of not letting my burn injury define me and the feeling that my body image was always on parade continued to cause internal conflict. Though most days found me too busy to dwell too deeply on these new aspects of my life, they hovered under the surface constantly.

Surprisingly, my give-back-for-a-year plan escalated upward for more than half a decade. The grant I received had enough funds for a four-year commitment. Though I took it one year at a time with my leave of absences from teaching, the day came when my principal needed to either replace me as a full-time teacher or bring me back into the fold. In 1986, he asked me to make a decision. It felt scary to cut the teaching tie and rely on grant money that had an end point. I knew I would be taking a risk. The deciding factor was the momentum of my new career and the impact I saw taking place before my eyes.

I presented a research paper about school reentry at the American Burn Association annual meeting in 1985, and the vision slowly began to catch the interest of surgeons and medical professionals who saw the importance of the vision. The fact that I was a teacher and a survivor added to the uniqueness and potential effectiveness of the program. Only a handful of survivors in the eighties attended the ABA meetings. Most of us who did were met with skepticism and curiosity about why we were even there. The culture of the ABA had a patriarchal hierarchy that did not recognize the voice nor the potential contribution of the survivor community. It would take years for us to achieve credibility. The school reentry program had tremendous potential to spread and needed to be established as a standard of care in every burn center. The ABA was the primary avenue for this to happen in order for kids all over the country to reenter school.

Being caught up in helping children gave me a purpose that motivated. I enjoyed the contact with kids and teens. Mideighties culture surrounded me with its fashionable big poofy hair and loads of hairspray. Denim jackets with neon T-shirts and Converse All-Star sneakers were popular for my school reentry kids. My hairpiece didn't allow for a high degree of poof, but I found ways to dress with style and fit in. If I was still lonely on a Saturday night, I squashed down the disappointment, the unknowns about my future, and focused on all the other things I was grateful for.

I created a social network, and though I didn't see myself as someone who would ever have a serious relationship again, I was carving out a worthwhile life in spite of it. Being a self-help book junkie allowed me a pathway to grow. I constantly tried to understand my inner world and analyze where I was heading.

When the grant expired, a new and exciting job opportunity was offered to me by a major Los Angeles County rehabilitation facility, Rancho Los Amigos Medical Center, and I didn't hesitate. I knew the Burn Rehabilitation director, Dr. Brody, from the early vetting process with my grant. A good portion of the kids I helped came from Rancho referrals. I had often attended rounds there during my grant years. The social worker and the director of pediatrics were both huge proponents of my work. The facility had a cutting-edge reputation and was one of the premier rehabilitation centers in the country at the time. Rancho hired me to do school reentry for their patients, but my job description reinvented itself on a daily basis.

I was lowest of the low on the medical specialties totem pole, yet thanks to a woman with administrative authority who truly believed in my program, a lovely large office space was granted to me. It proved very useful as the scope of my work increased. The center gave me the freedom to be as innovative and creative as I could to provide community reentry interventions to benefit patients. With twenty-three specialties, Rancho treated more medical issues than burns. I was thrust into a world I had no comprehension nor former knowledge of, the world of cleft palate, lupus, Möbius and Treacher Collins syndromes, craniosynostosis, and scleroderma. Most of these rare disorders left men, women, and children with some type of a facial difference.

It was overwhelming. Each specialty had its own individual progression and unique treatment plan, often complicated by other health issues. Hiding became a way of life for far too many, staying home during the day and only venturing out to shop when stores emptied of customers late in the evening. People could slink in under the cover of darkness, quickly gather what they needed, and melt back into oblivion.

Rancho was committed to do more than the usual "treat 'em and street 'em." Aftercare mattered. Patients walked into my office, sat down in my chair, and displayed what they struggled with: discolored skin, scars, misshapen features, hair loss, and amputations. They came with common body image themes.

"I'm so tired of being stared at. I've stopped going to church and my card club because of it."

"I can't believe that people feel they can just walk up and ask me any time and any place about my burns!"

"No one is going to hire me looking like this."

"My daughter gets picked on at school every day. What can we do?"

"I can hide all of the scars on my body except for the ones on my face. Please help."

I felt their emotional pain. I wanted to be an encouragement. I wanted to give them tools that would make a difference. With this quality-of-life rehab focus, the center's goals meshed with mine. I was thrilled to be part of the process.

Mostly.

There was the day Dr. Brody approached me with a new assignment. What he lacked in height, Dr. Brody made up for with a commanding voice and demeanor that gave you an instant realization that he was whip-smart but also unerringly kind and approachable.

"Barbara, I have been thinking it would be a good idea for you to figure out a way to teach our patients about how to use makeup to help them feel better. It's a service we need to offer to improve their self-image."

I gave him my raised-eyebrows-concerned-stare look. "You seriously want me to teach makeup techniques?" I asked.

He nodded his head.

I shook mine.

Granted, I highly respected the man for his genuine concern for patients and his attentive bedside manner. His request shouldn't have surprised me. But didn't he know this was a skill far out of my repertoire of tools? I had struggled to learn to use the strategies and tools to "normalize" my face by restoring my skin to one color, drawing on eyebrows and a symmetrical lip line. I had no skills and no clue how to assist others.

I must also confess it seemed a bit beneath my educator status at this particular point in my career. For my hesitant attitude, I was jettisoned to advanced makeup school.

Not too thrilled with my assignment, the first day of the two-week training had me entirely out of my element and found lacking. Who knew there were so many skin tones, nuances of color, techniques, brushes, applications? Around twenty of us listened to lectures all morning, and we then entered a lab for the real work in the afternoons.

The instructor, a generously proportioned middle-aged man, came from a well-known Hollywood makeup artist family. He should have been a drill sergeant in the US Army. It was as if he had to prepare us for DEFCON 3, with imminent danger to unenhanced skin. He jumped from station to station, shouting his praise or dissatisfaction, mostly the latter.

"No. No. No, Barbara. You have to sweep upward with the brush stroke—*sweep*!"

I tried not to roll my eyes. I followed his directive, mumbling to myself, "You're enduring this for the patients, for the patients…"

By the end of the first day, happy hour never had such appeal. A group of us with the same frame of mind ventured out to rehash the day. A true whine fest.

Nine more days of my head spinning, and the tyrant demanding, to look forward to.

But in the end, my tool kit grew. And I began to see him as more benevolent than tyrant, wanting the best to help me with my job. Unlike me, most of my seminar classmates came from the esthetician field and had some experience with makeup. As a complete novice, teaching me had been an extra challenge.

Back at Rancho with my new skills, I felt a little sorry for the patients I first attempted to transform with my rookie makeup techniques. My motivation centered on the difference I knew it could make, even though it would take years to craft my art on the myriad of faces I encountered. Maria was my first "experiment," one of my extremely kind and patient Hispanic clients. She walked in on a Monday morning for my first appointment of the day, poking her head into my office.

"Maria, I'm so glad to see you. Come on in and have a seat. I hope you are ready to try some new makeup," I said, directing her to the swivel chair in front of a large lighted mirror.

"*Si*, Barbara, *si*."

Maria was burned in a house fire that left moderate scarring on her cheeks. Partly because she declined to wear the pressure garments, she had some raised and thick scar lines, along with discoloration, in several areas.

"Okay, Maria, to begin with, I'm going to find just the right shade for your skin tone…"

Looking at the various scars and trying not to panic, I quickly scanned my collection of base colors. Aida Gray had made this part look so easy when she first worked with me back in beauty wonderland. I appreciated her skill now more than ever.

I chose a few I thought might blend the diverse areas. The color had to first harmonize with the original tone of her neck, and then match the rest of the area up to her cheeks.

"Let's try this one."

"Or maybe that one."

"Or maybe?"

After fumbling for the right color for twenty minutes, she had ten sample shades lining her jaw, five on each side. My lips pursed, grimacing at my handiwork. But I refused to give up. If I could bless Maria a portion of how Aida blessed me, the DEFCON training would have been worth it.

Thankfully, Maria was highly invested in the process and didn't show signs of impatience or doubting me. Once we thought we had found the right shade, we worked together to apply the makeup. The goal of the day was for Maria to learn how to use the products to repeat the process at home. I showed her how to dab on the makeup with a sponge, and she took over. We were both pleased at the difference the base color made. The former blotchy patches looked smoother, deemphasizing the scar lines. We powdered to set the makeup, and then added lip liner and lipstick as a finishing component. We played with blush colors and a little eye shadow. Her sweet smile at the end of our session said it all.

"Barbara, *buen trabajo*. Thank you." She hugged me and walked out the door with one last glance in the mirror, her eyes bright and appreciative. She also walked out with a set of products free of charge, thanks to a generous fund I could access. Purchasing replacements would cost a nominal price when she ran out. Compared to the subpar makeup found in the mall that was often pasty and cakey, the private-label products we used were of much higher quality and more user friendly.

I knew in my heart I had passed on an enormous tool, one that would help Maria minimize the intrusion of stares and unwanted attention. She left with a new level of confidence about herself and more ready to face the world.

My beginning successes put me on the hunt for more ways to help. I first saw the effects of color analysis at an American Burn Association meeting during the Burn Survivor Special Interest Group session. The presenter draped different colors of fabric over the chest and around the shoulders of a female survivor with significant facial scars and skin discoloration. The results astonished me. Colors that were harmonious with her skin tone, eyes, and hair color diminished the visibility of scars, asymmetry, and discoloration. Nonharmonious colors heightened the scars and skin discoloration, emphasizing her facial difference.

The color of the fabrics used were divided first by undertones, whether warm or cool, and then by vividness. Seeing firsthand the dramatic effect of wearing the right colors, I knew I needed to incorporate this new aspect of image enhancement into my tool kit as well as into my personal life.

This training took only five days, but challenged me more than the makeup classes ever did. It takes a trained eye and discernment to pick the undertone of a person's skin. The color artist has to analyze three factors: skin tone, eye color, and one's natural hair color. The three of them together determine tone and vividness. If a natural blonde dyes her hair red, the color artist has to cover the hair to determine the undertone. If a person has dark brown eyes, the undertone is cool, but if the eyes are brown with amber and gold flecks, the undertone leans toward warm.

I entertained the idea of dropping out halfway through, but again the thought of our patients, the team, and Dr. Brody kept me fighting to learn such an important-though-complicated tool. If wearing the right colors could de-accentuate scars, then spending money on the right wardrobe was paramount.

In 1988, I gave the new work a more formal name and titled it "The Image Enhancement Program." From time to time, I was given opportunities to speak to small groups on this topic, along with facing the public with a facial difference. I was invited to support groups, a college nursing program, the Cleft Palate Association, and an international burn conference, to name a few. Even local groups such as the Rotary Club and other philanthropic organizations heard about my presentation and asked me to speak.

The concepts I shared went all the way back to my first dinner out at Marie Callender's with Bobby and Judy after leaving the hospital. Shoulders back. Walk proudly. Don't let them see you sweat. I added in ideas from the self-help books from the eighties. *8 Steps to Powerful Living* by Dr. Frank Freed influenced my self-talk and perception of my injuries. Dr. Freed lost an arm in World War II and became a Baptist minister after returning home. He eventually earned his PhD and became the director of counseling at the Crystal Cathedral. He was a powerful motivational speaker, and I often attended his lectures. He eventually became a friend and life coach. He emphasized positive living and thinking differently about life-altering events with faith and a good attitude.

Sharing the tools forced me to consolidate my ideas into useful snippets. One morning I was sitting at my dining room table working on a presentation for a small Phoenix Society regional conference in Southern California. The Phoenix Society was a young start-up organization founded by Alan Breslau, whose mission was to connect burn survivors with each other. I mulled over the importance of helping people understand how their behavioral skills influenced the kind of reaction they received from others. I lifted up a prayer,

God, how can I teach this in a simple and easy-to-remember way so survivors feel more comfortable and in control out in public?

I kept brainstorming, searching for a clear framework that people would connect with and easily remember. While composing possible ideas on a yellow legal pad, five concepts suddenly popped into my head: self-talk, tone of voice, eye contact, posture, and smile.

STEPS was born.

Thank You, Lord, for this gift!

118

What we say *to* ourselves *about* ourselves and believe creates our reality and how we handle life. Our tone of voice projects either capability and confidence, or weakness and insecurity. Eye contact conveys that we are comfortable with ourselves and open to connecting with other people. Good posture projects pride and inner strength. A smile communicates joy, approachability, sincerity, and as a bonus, softens one's facial difference, fostering a connection with another person.

They seem simple, and yet anyone benefits from using STEPS, whether a person lives with scars, sits in a wheelchair, or uses a prosthesis. Even someone self-conscious about a blemish can use it.

I tried to think creatively about my teaching methods, wanting to demonstrate the use of my new tool. For the Phoenix Society conference, I donned a dress that wasn't the right color for me and out of proportion for my body. I also wore not-so-flattering accessories. After a glowing and positive introduction by the coordinator of the event with the promise of life-changing methods, I walked up to the podium with my head bowed down, a mousy wig hanging haphazardly about my face. Making no eye contact and mumbling my words into the microphone, I told the group I was there to speak on how to "up your self-esteem."

I could see out of the corner of my eye the puzzled looks and concern of the audience turning to pity. My final words to them set up the next section of my talk.

"And I'm sure you are wondering after that glowing introduction why I was chosen as your speaker…"

And then the music from *The Stripper* loudly boomed from big speakers. I slowly chucked off the wig, belt, and lackluster dress and threw them into the crowd, revealing an attractive, color-coordinated, and well-fitting outfit underneath. Pausing for the gasps of shock and laughter to cease, along with the applause and catcalls, I confidently reintroduced myself and began to share about image enhancement and STEPS. The contrast itself drove home the power a burn survivor has to garner positive responses from the public through their own behavioral and social skills.

I loved my job.

I added other tools along my teaching path. Rehearse your responses (RYR) was developed due to complaints of constant and intrusive questions. From my own encounters, I had learned the value of a three-sentence answer, one on the tip of my tongue that I could deliver in an awkward situation to change the dynamics of the interaction. I would often say, "I was burned in a car crash. I'm doing better now. Thanks for your concern." If they prodded for more information, I would set my boundary by saying, "That's all I want to discuss now. I hope you understand." Then with a smile, I would go about my business.

When I first started talking to people about my injury, I felt I needed to give the long version, as if I owed every stranger in the universe the details of my life. My friend Judy and I were at a store one day, and a fellow customer asked me, "Have you recently had a face lift? Is that why your face looks drawn and tight?"

Judy and I looked at each other and started to laugh. I answered the curious woman, shaking my head. "No, I wish it were that simple. I had a burn injury from a car crash..."

And off I went, going into great detail about what happened to me and why I wore the mask. The horrified look on the woman's face kept me rambling for many long minutes, trying to calm the tension my words raised. To no avail. I finally ended the conversation rather abruptly, and we walked away.

After numerous uncomfortable and tiring conversations such as this one, I became cognizant of my behavior and began questioning my obligation to share so much. I made a conscious decision to lighten my load. I determined to *succinctly* share when I was burned, how I was doing at the moment, and thank the person for their concern.

I taught this RYR technique of having a short and concise answer to a group of kids at the Denver Children's Hospital Burn Camp one summer. They held their camp at Cheley in Estes Park, a beautiful spot in the Rocky Mountains. The director of the camp, Marion Doctor, LCSW, developed the first therapeutic and recreational burn camp in the nation. Her camp served as a model for other camps that have been developed throughout the country, Canada, and Europe. Burn camps offer kids a week of adventure, socializing, gaining confidence and skills, and good old-fashioned fun. They don't have to hide their scars or be embarrassed by their appearance. Kids can just be themselves among their peers who understand. Life-long friendships are formed. Marion's legacy and visionary idea has impacted thousands of young burn survivors throughout the world.

At one particular teaching session, the ages of the campers greatly varied, and I struggled to hold the attention of the six- and seven-year-olds along with the teenagers. I had a group of young boys with short attention spans sitting around my ankles, kicking each other, poking, making faces, only half listening to me. I managed to get through the presentation, but doubted that it had impacted the distracted boys in any way.

A month later, one of the boys' parents called and asked what happened at camp. Their son Jeremy hadn't been dealing well with his anger when he encountered people out in public. The stares and comments had been inciting him to lash out physically and verbally. But after his time at burn camp, they noticed a big change in him. In the grocery store one day, the bag boy at the checkout counter saw Jeremy's scars and had the nerve to pull aside his collar and exclaim, "Man, what happened?"

While Jeremy's mom braced herself for the explosion, she heard her son calmly say instead, "I was burned two years ago. I'm doing great now. Thanks for asking."

He didn't get angry and just walked off with a spring in his step.

If a seven-year-old could gain from the half-listened-to Rehearse Your Responses tool, I knew I was on the right track.

The staring tool evolved in a similar fashion. Survivors struggle with how to react when strangers gawk or give double takes, even triple takes. I instructed kids how to confidently control any interaction by smiling and confidently saying, "Hi, how are ya doin'?" or "Hi, isn't it a great day?"

Speaking in a friendly tone of voice is the easiest and fastest way to stop an uncomfortable moment, allowing someone to see you as a person rather than focusing on a scar, a prosthesis, or wheelchair. Making eye contact and hearing a voice turns attention away from the physical to the inner person. It helps people see the survivor as a person rather than an object.

I needed the tools as much as anyone, which made it more real for my patients. Knowing I was a walking demonstration motivated me to create my own style. Body image plays a huge role in our self-identity and feelings of worth. I had been self-conscious about my weight since my teenage years. Like most women, I struggled and longed for approval and acceptance. Getting used to the addition of scars was a painstakingly slow process. I didn't mind showing my calves by wearing mid-knee shorts at this point, but I still tended to hide my back. I envied women who could wear low-back blouses and sleeveless tops.

These pangs hit me at times. I looked longingly at a friend's manicure or saw a tennis match, and a little dagger poked my heart. I had to fight for perspective, to remember the thousands of things I could still do instead of the few things I couldn't.

The pangs are a natural part of ongoing recovery and a life-long step-by-step adjustment, but I truly believe the tools play a big role. My scars didn't lessen, but my self-consciousness and vigilance about people staring at me did. The tools could help make recovery a possibility. And I wanted to share them with the world.

11

Dreams

"Thunder only happens when it's raining. Players only love you when they're playing..."

I switched the radio off, my usual habit whenever "Dreams" by Fleetwood Mac played its lamenting tune across the airwaves. The song has haunted me since my accident a decade ago. Unbidden, the lyrics I didn't want to remember sounded in my head:

Dreams of loneliness like a heartbeat, drives you mad
In the stillness of remembering
What you had and what you lost

It felt like I was no longer a player.

My friend Judy was in the car with me. Ironically, we were on our way to a mutual friend's wedding. Newly divorced, Judy understood the pain of lost relationships.

"Judy, I miss dating. I miss flirting. I never imagined that I'd spend the rest of life alone. Why does it seem like women can accept the scars of their partners so much more readily than men?"

"I'm afraid to answer that. My cynicism is running pretty high right now. Let's just stay positive and assume there are some great men out there who can handle scars. And real emotions. It just seems impossible to find them."

"But don't forget, we only need one good man each," I said with a smile, wondering if or when that would ever be a reality.

We both sighed. A silence fell between us.

"It can't be just about looks," I said. "We have some attractive friends who are single and some average-looking ones who are married."

Judy hesitated and then affirmed, "Isn't that the irony of life?"

"I just want the choice, ya know?" I said. "I keep remembering an old friend's words, that perhaps a nice disabled man will come along someday who will be interested in me…Not that I wouldn't mind a great man like that, but are my options limited to someone else with an injury?"

"No. I'm totally offended by that comment. It almost has a prejudicial tone. It's as if people can't overcome the idea that someone's body difference limits them to only one path. Murray and your wretched ex did your self-esteem no favors. Don't give up so quickly…"

I had thought myself deeply in love with Murray. When the relationship died, the pain of the breakup was, in some ways, as devastating as the change in my appearance. It meant a drastic blow to my social life and how I saw myself as a woman. I had always had a boyfriend in my life. Not that Murray had been so fabulous, but I understood that he wouldn't easily be replaced.

That inner romantic yearning to love and be loved had stayed alive in me. I determined to value and pursue the relationships I already had in my life and go from there. Hanging out with friends, whether single or married, has never bothered me. A social life was a social life, and I loved connecting with people. I had come to a point in my recovery where I wasn't focusing so much on myself. My job at

Rancho Los Amigos connected me with a vibrant medical team. I had the opportunity to develop community reentry programs not just for children, but also with adults to help them get back to life. Every day there could be a new surprise or something to learn, and creativity had no bounds in how we developed innovative interventions to assist our patients. I was happy with my life and the path I was on. The lingering dreams that I had, I kept close to my heart.

If my accident has taught me anything, it had to be that everything started with my own inner contentment about my life, my identity, and my relationships. I had to approach all this from a position of strength and a sense of worth. I had gained the monumental skill of confidence and social control in my life through the skills I learned. My life was by no means complete. I had dreams yet to realize.

I had much to give.

With the self-help boom of the late eighties all around me, I signed up for a seminar on personal development. I figured that if I wanted to be with a healthy partner, I needed to work on myself to attract that kind of person. I made a list of qualities I thought important in a husband. I didn't choose the shallow stuff. I wanted someone with an admirable character and quality values in harmony with mine. I wanted him to have a career he enjoyed, be wise with finances, and love and treat his family well. He should enjoy life and like social events. He had to be supportive of my work and mission, though he didn't have to participate in everything.

I tried not to include good grammar on the list, but to my chagrin, it got added. A non-teacher would have had very different ideas of what was sexy in a partner, but *that was me*. He certainly didn't have to be 6'1" and perfect. My previous choices had involved more cake than meat. This time around, I needed someone stable and solid.

Of course, I was not sure how I was going to meet someone who fulfilled my list. My dating queue was at zero. I consoled myself with the thought that a man could get to know me first as a friend or colleague. A dating relationship could blossom from there. It was one thing to mouth those words, however, and a whole other reality to believe them. Fighting my own insecurities, I thought positively as I entered the workshop doors.

The ballroom of a local hotel hosted the weekend seminar. Chairs lined up in rows awaited my seating choice. A mix of men and women were there, patiently thumbing through the folders handed to them on the way in. I grabbed a chair close to the front and perused the materials. The schedule for the day involved several lectures on one's self-talk and communication skills. Time was given between lectures for exercises, questions, and debate among the participants. I settled in for a long day, hoping for some good nuggets to take away with me.

After a lecture on self-talk, the leader gave us a writing assignment.

"Our next exercise is for you to choose a topic dear to you and then write down an affirming statement. Make sure you use present tense as if it is already fact. This is part of your becoming..."

Dating was a topic very dear to my heart. I picked up my pen and started to form thoughts, line after line flowing out of my pen. By the end of the session, I had reduced the flow to these few words:

I am a loving and lovable physically and emotionally attractive woman who is worthy of a successful and happy Christian marriage.

Satisfied with my affirmation, I stuffed the blue 3×5 card in my purse. At the moment, I was far from feeling those words deep in my soul, but I wanted to change my self-talk and believe my message in every cell of my body. When negative thoughts arose, I pulled the affirmation out and reminded myself of my goal to think and feel differently. I committed myself and any future dates to prayer. I asked God to help me choose wisely. I knew that I wouldn't ever have men knocking down my door to date me, but I only needed *one good man*. With that resolved in my heart and mind, I went on with living my life and pursuing meaning.

If I found myself still checking men for wedding rings, it was a normal pursuit for any single gal, right? I needed to keep my heart open and not let cynicism close it down.

I am a loving and lovable…

I love how God can use the mundane.

I got a phone call one day from a man named Ken.

"Barbara Kammerer?"

"Yes."

"My name is Ken Quayle, and I'm the president of your home owner's association [HOA]. We have been getting complaints about your renters regarding noise and constant partying…again! Please address these issues as soon as possible."

I had been renting out a condo I purchased years back while teaching. The income generated helped me financially, but the hassles kept piling up. My renters often made it to the top of the *seriously annoying* list of the HOA board of directors.

"I'm so sorry, Ken. I will call them…Actually, I have been thinking for a while now that I should sell that unit. If you hear of any buyers poking around the place, please let me know."

"I can do better than that. I know of a new couple who are looking. I will give them a call and get back to you."

I liked his voice. And I remembered him from my time living in the condo, but the extent of our interaction was saying hello in passing.

I met up with Ken face-to-face a few months later on the day I signed the final paperwork to sell the unit. He was forty-something, five feet ten inches tall, and handsome with kind hazel eyes. No wedding ring. And I owed the man a serious thank-you. I ran through my options. Flowers? Guys hate flowers. Sports tickets? Expensive. Food? Sounded like the simplest idea.

I made a plan to take him out to dinner, chat it up for an hour or so, and get some extra sleep on a Sunday night. Perfect.

I chose an Italian restaurant close to the condo complex. Fiorito had been around for decades, offering the locals casual dining and mouthwatering pasta choices. The dim lighting and ma-and-pa simple decor made for a cozy atmosphere. Black-and-white photos of local celebrities smiling with the owner lined the entrance wall.

The hostess seated Ken and me in a booth near the front window framed with lace curtains. I was not nervous, per se, but a one-to-one dinner with a man I barely knew felt a bit awkward at first.

To my surprise, our conversation flowed effortlessly, and we found ourselves lingering over decaf coffee and life stories far longer than I had expected. I learned that Ken had two children from a former marriage, a son who was sixteen and a daughter in her early twenties. His pride over their accomplishments came across in a sweet way. He had worked at ABC Television in Hollywood as an audio engineer for years. Ken showed himself to be an affable, intelligent man who was easy to talk to. We kept the conversation off of the deeply personal, but found we had a lot in common.

The evening ended with a quick hug and a hope-to-see-you-again-sometime vibe. A pure friendship grew slowly over the next months, mostly through prolonged phone calls. Rancho Los Amigos was a catalyst for launching my Image Enhancement and Aftercare Programs in other burn centers across the country. I found myself traveling a lot, but fit in the occasional casual lunch with Ken. With both of us having failed marriages behind us, neither of us was in any rush to commit to a long-term relationship. Having fun together brought a new joy into my life that I had been dreaming about. I didn't dwell on the risk. The longing of my heart overrode wariness.

Ken thought me fragile, as if my scars would cause pain if he touched them. I divested him of the misconception quickly, though like most women, my feelings could be hurt and cause pain far more easily than his. Out in public together, he noticed people staring at me at times and marveled that I didn't react in a negative manner. But truthfully, when I was with someone, I rarely noticed the stares. I was totally enveloped in the social moment. And even when alone, I chose not to focus on the stares, pushing them off-radar almost unconsciously. At some point, I realized I had become overly vigilant about this. It was freeing to let go of the need to see if people were staring. I became tired of letting what I thought other people were thinking of me rule my life. While having a man at my side did give me an added feeling of security, I didn't need to cling to him to feel okay about my existence. I was making progress in a way that I hadn't before.

With time, I was ready for more. Something permanent. My heart had become further and further involved. I didn't get a sense from Ken, however, that he felt the same way. While I knew he cared about me, he avoided talking about our future, even though he spent all his free time with me.

At dinner one evening, he timidly broached the subject. "Barbara, you know I really care about you, but I'm not sure I can make a commitment. I can only hope you are okay with that…I would really like for us to keep seeing each other, maybe even live together someday."

Seeing the writing on the wall, I looked him straight in the eye and mustered the courage to say, "That's really tough to hear, Ken. You know me well enough to understand that I would never agree to just live with you."

I have always believed that women sell themselves short and give away power by moving in with their boyfriends. I know it sounds old-fashioned, but I believe taking vows before God and legally sealing a commitment changes the fabric of what holds two people together.

"Ken, I think we would be great together. Even though I don't like how you feel, I have to accept it. I think it is better for me to move on. I really want to be married someday."

Heart-wrenching words to voice.

The sound of a dream dying.

I woke up every morning for a few months afterward, and I grieved. Life felt unfair all over again, and I fought to avoid feeling devastated. The thought of starting again with someone else when I knew Ken and I could be great together exhausted me. The bigger question loomed: would I ever find anyone else? Ken was the first serious relationship I had had since my accident.

I pulled out my affirmation.

I am a loving and lovable…who is worthy…

One good man. He could still be out there. But I had to let go of Ken.

With Murray I had felt helpless and hopeless. But with Ken, I had a different perspective because I was at a stronger point in my life.

And because of my experience with Ken, I learned some things. I realized that it wasn't about being a player. Beauty truly is in the eye of the beholder. Great guys who can handle scars exist. They can be found. There are just no guarantees in life. It all came back to God and me, being okay with who I was and where I was heading in life. I had purpose. I had a lot of friends, and I was okay.

I committed myself to letting go. And moving forward.

* * *

I love how God unexpectedly works sometimes.

Several months after our breakup, I was talking to a friend on the phone. Ken's name came up, and she wanted me to know that he had a new grandchild. His daughter, Jennifer, whom I adored, had a new baby girl. I was thrilled for the family. After thinking about it for a few days, I decided to give Ken a quick phone call to congratulate him. I bore no grudges. Ken would always have a little piece of my heart.

He answered on the first ring.

"Ken, I hear congratulations are in order. I am so happy for you. How is Jennifer?"

"Thanks, Barbara. Mom and baby are doing fine. She and David named their baby girl Heather. She is healthy with a good set of lungs. Her parents are getting used to a whole new lifestyle than the one they had before, to say the least."

We talked for a long time, catching up with each other. The conversation took a more serious turn as we brought up the topic of our relationship.

"Barbara, I really miss seeing you. Can we get together and talk over dinner sometime?"

His words struck me as being deeply sincere. And at some level, I really wanted to see him too. Maybe our time apart had him thinking more deeply about our relationship.

"What about your fears of a permanent commitment? Can you get past them?"

"I don't know, but I really want to try. With time and help, maybe I can."

Jokes about couples in therapy run rampant, but our sessions together with a counselor unearthed some pain in Ken's past that had to be dealt with. Gaining clarity and the perspective that I was not the same woman as his ex-wife made all the difference. The healing began. It gave us both the hope that we could someday be great together.

A few months after our final counseling session, I invited Ken and his brother Riley and sister-in-law Diane over for dinner. I loved to cook and often entertained guests at my home. I was busy in the kitchen when I heard the doorbell. Ken walked in with a magnificent crystal vase filled with pink long-stemmed roses and proudly set them on my coffee table. He wore a mischievous smile on his face as we sat down on the sofa together. Giving him a hug and kiss of appreciation, I wondered what I had done to deserve such an extravagant and beautiful bouquet. Had I missed an important occasion? I carefully opened the small card and saw four words boldly written in cursive:

Will you marry me?

I was shocked. I was stunned.

I laughed and cried as I exuberantly responded, "Yes!"

We embraced each other for a long time and truly savored the moment.

The engagement ring came a little later. With my misshapen fingers, we decided a beautiful bracelet set with diamonds would take the place of a traditional band.

The wedding turned out to be a little untraditional too. We held it at an art museum with two dear friends performing the ceremony. Chaplain Jane Dubois had remained a dear friend since our time together through my mother's cancer. Dr. Frank Freed, a minister, friend, and life coach over the years was another heartfelt choice. Together, they brought together elements of my Catholic faith and Ken's spirituality.

I wore a long white elegant lace dress accented with sequins and pearls. I carried a dramatic bouquet of Casablanca lilies. My dear friend Judy was my maid of honor and Ken's daughter Jennifer my bridesmaid. In place of my father, I chose three dear men from my childhood—Nick, Bret, and Andy Carter—to walk me down the aisle. After my father's death, we grew even closer to the Carter family. I considered them the brothers I never had. It seemed fitting that they play a significant role in this very special day. Nick's little daughter and my godchild, Justine, all dressed in pink, was our beautiful flower girl. Daniel, the son of my dear friend Mary Ellen, served as our ring bearer and looked very handsome in his tuxedo.

We shared our vows before loving friends and family, who expressed tremendous joy and support for our union. Dr. Freed's vibrant voice brought tears when he described our relationship with the words "You do for me what sunlight does for stained glass…"

I felt beautiful. Inside and out.

After a lovely al fresco patio lunch and dancing with our guests, Ken and I stole away for our first night together along the Newport Beach coast.

No thunder, no rain…only a dream coming true.

With Ken, I experienced a sense of total acceptance. He didn't try to control me or mold me into some other image. He saw *me*, not my burn injury. I didn't fear being abandoned for lack of perfection or some change in my appearance. I didn't have to be vigilant about every action or word spoken. We committed ourselves to each other, both in it for the long haul…forever.

Being married to Ken, I gained a new set of parents to love and cherish. His children and their families became a special part of my life. One good man brought me more than I had dreamed about. To this day, Ken is one of the smartest people I have ever known. He has a calm and rational demeanor that complements my energetic and sometimes overstimulated personality. While we have some interests we don't share, there are many that we do. It adds balance to our relationship and exposes each to new horizons.

And his grammar—*impeccable.*

12

Inroads

The bus meandered along US Route 40 on the outskirts of St. Louis. Burnt orange leaves blew across our path, their cheery counterparts still dangling from green and white ash trees lining the road. The sunny October day in 1993 set the perfect mood for reflection. I was there with fellow survivors for a conference sponsored by the Phoenix Society. A burn survivor named Alan Breslau founded the organization in 1977, the same year as my car crash. He had been burned during the sixties in a commercial airline catastrophe. He was inspired to found the organization after visiting a young boy at a burn center in Pennsylvania and seeing the need for peer support. I learned about the organization through the American Burn Association in the early eighties and lent my support over the years.

About two hundred of us were on our way to a barbecue outside the city. That morning I had spoken at the plenary session on image enhancement. My presentation showcased the benefits of skilled makeup use and the wise choice of clothing to minimize the appearance of scars. I showed some of my own pictures and makeovers of other survivors I had worked with at Rancho. I hoped the information would prove useful for many of our attendees. The barbecue provided a chance to mingle and meet new acquaintances.

"Barbara, I have been wanting to meet you. My name is Amy Acton. I am a burn survivor and burn nurse at Blodgett in Grand Rapids. Thanks for sharing this morning."

The woman sitting next to me had short black hair and warm chocolate brown eyes with an engaging smile to accompany them.

"It's nice to meet you, Amy. What did you think of the session?"

"Well, to be truthful, I have kind of always thought that wearing makeup for a survivor is like hiding, pretending something isn't there that really is. Does that make any sense?"

I noticed that she had not a speck of makeup on her smooth cheeks, lips, and eyelids. The only visible scarring I could see were skin grafts on the right side of her neck. Her comment didn't offend me. I realized not every woman deemed makeup a necessity for her appearance.

"Well, to me it is just a tool, like all of our tools. Most people have skin that is all one color, eyebrows, and a symmetrical lip line. If makeup can give that to a survivor and aid in community reentry, why not use it?" I said.

"A tool…I guess I have to think about it more. Makeup has never been on my personal radar much. But put like that, I see your point."

"So tell me a bit of your story, Amy. How were you injured?" I asked.

"Right after I graduated from high school, I worked at a marina for the summer. I was moving a twenty-foot skiff from one slip to another on the opposite side. The mast was taller than I realized, and it didn't clear the power line that gave us electricity. The voltage pulsed through my hand into the carotid artery of my neck. I almost bled out by the time someone found me. Thank god a police officer happened by. He called 911 and kept the bleeding under control until an ambulance got there."

"How bad was the damage?"

"I didn't have a high-percentage burn, but the injury went deep. My vocal cords suffered, and I had to have my hand and neck skin grafted."

"What do you do now?"

"I'm the nurse manager at the burn center at Blodgett Hospital in Grand Rapids, Michigan. I've been working there for several years, and I love the job."

Meeting survivors who invest their careers in helping new burn patients always encouraged me.

We went on to chat more about her journey as a survivor and as a nurse in Grand Rapids. I sensed she was a leader. Amy had driven a van-load of ten survivors from her burn center to the conference. I appreciated her commitment to aftercare. I wished we had dozens more like her, survivors bridging the gap between the medical and recovery worlds.

Making inroads.

I must have given her food for thought regarding the makeup issue. A couple months later, I got a call from her asking me to fly to Grand Rapids and present a training for image enhancement and my community reentry tools, now called the Behavioral Enhancement Skills Training (BEST) program at her burn center. I planned for a four-day event. The first day I taught the behavioral skills for navigating the public to a group of six staff members. The next two days focused on demonstrating the basic makeup techniques. For the final day, a group of burn survivors were invited to the hospital. They acted as models for the staff to receive hands-on experience, imparting the skills they had learned.

Amy joined me for dinner at my hotel each night after our sessions with the staff. We bonded over a shared love of food, spicy entrees paired with delicious wines. The chance to debrief and talk shop sealed our friendship. On the last evening, we branched out and ended up at her favorite tapas restaurant downtown. I wanted to know her thoughts on the program and plans for the future.

"Amy, have you heard any feedback from the staff on the behavioral skills training? I'm curious to know how much they will implement the different elements. They seemed to be enthused."

"I know the exposure to the materials, especially the tools, has everyone thinking deeply about ways they can impact patients before they ever leave the hospital. It's not something we typically focus on. Sadly."

"Amy, it's like burn centers are in a coma of their own. I feel like we are making so little progress in this country to promote reentry programs after discharge."

"I agree it's discouraging. I find it hard to believe that most centers don't even offer a simple support group for survivors. Patients walk out the door and flounder, trying to adjust to life. No one talks about the challenges of what awaits them at home and out in public. No one prepares them for how hard it is to get back to school or to work."

"I'm always stunned when I run into people who have gone for years having never met another survivor after their injuries," I said. "My occupational therapist connected me with a male survivor after my injury, but I didn't meet any women with facial burns rivaling mine for years. I would have loved to talk to someone as I progressed through my surgeries. There is definitely a huge piece missing in the rehab process. What we are doing in this training is a step in the right direction, but we have so far to go for it to be a standard of care. Reaching one center at a time with a few staff feels like a drop in an ocean of need."

"And how do we get more survivors helping survivors? Some kind of peer support system happening? That's my big question," Amy said.

"The Phoenix Society is a great idea, offering support to survivors and their families, but it is just too small and has many limitations," I said. "The medical world doesn't seem to respect the organization enough to foster any kind of impact."

"I wish we could change that, but it seems more than daunting," Amy acknowledged.

We agreed that it was pioneering work, attempting to make inroads for aftercare. My passion for the programs stemmed from my own experience, wanting no one else to leave the safe world of the hospital walls having never seen their new face or having never been given any social skills tools to help them adjust and cope.

Research reflected how people's reaction to a facial difference was more severe than for those with a physical impairment, such as an uneven gait or amputation. I had met people with many types of facial and body differences struggling deeply with social exclusion and their need to belong unfulfilled. So many beautiful souls' quality of life had been diminished for lack of training and support to overcome this great challenge.

An advocate colleague of mine from Israel, Dahlia Gilboa, PhD, wrote an article with the premise of a conspiracy of avoidance among burn professionals. She theorized that there was a code of silence in burn centers that let the staff off the hook. If no one talked about the painful reality a patient would face outside the walls, then they didn't have to feel the weight of responsibility for helping patients with their community reentry.

Just because a patient wasn't talking about the hard questions didn't mean he or she wasn't thinking about them.

Constantly.

I had a running list in my head of my own thoughts after the accident. *How am I going to go back to work? Be out in a crowd at an event or wander a mall? No one is ever going to love me like this. Who would ever want to hold my hand? Kiss me? Be intimate with me?*

The excuses burn professionals gave for not addressing these issues ran the gamut:

"We don't have the time or resources for aftercare."

"We can barely handle in-house psychology issues, let alone focus on future ones."

"We can only treat the physical wounds. It is up to the patient to move on with their lives."

Excuses all. So much more could be done. And needed to be done.

It was no longer enough to save someone's life and send them on their not-so-merry way unprepared. I advocated *saying the hard truth softly*. It was vital to sit down with a patient surrounded by a loved one and a burn care professional to talk about the changes in their appearance.

During my time at Rancho, I had been asked more than once to come to various burn centers and help a patient look in the mirror for the first time. I had no magical formula. The emotional impact hit me harder than perhaps a more objective burn professional. It requires great courage for anyone.

Amy and I saw the need and, partially, the solution. The barriers came with rallying the burn world, especially the medical sphere, to our cause.

Hearing about struggling survivors reemphasized all our concerns about the state of aftercare. Wherever I went, conversations were often struck about someone knowing someone with a burn injury and how I really needed to meet them. It was flattering to be in the position of advocate but also overwhelming at times to meet another's tragedy face-to-face.

A young woman came to my attention through a friend of a friend. At age twenty-six, she had been a regional sales rep for a large pharmaceutical company in the Midwest. A beautiful young woman, she was climbing the corporate ladder with steady steam when her injury occurred. One Saturday morning she decided to use some gasoline on her tire rims to clean them properly. Having finished the task, she brought the near-empty gas can into her apartment and set it next to a pilot light for a water heater in the hallway. When the heater kicked in, the fumes ignited and exploded, leaving her severely burned—face, hands, and body.

I flew to the Midwest to consult with her two years after she initially left the hospital. We met at my hotel. It wasn't difficult to find each other in the busy lobby. Our obvious scars drew us together like a homing device. We found a private room to meet in. She seemed eager to talk to another woman with a burn injury, someone who could empathize with her story.

She had had no further reconstructive surgeries done on her face after her initial stay at the hospital. Her hands were barely functional, her posture hunched from the scar tissue. The grafts on her neck had contracted so severely that her lower lip, cheeks, and even her eyelids looked contorted, pulled down from their normal positions.

I thought carefully before I said, "Is there a reason why you haven't undergone some reconstructive surgeries to release some of these tight areas?"

"Barbara, I keep hitting a brick wall trying to get help. My company is willing to pay for more treatment, but I just don't know where to turn. At my last appointment with my surgeon, I told him how depressed I am."

"Did he have any advice?" I asked.

"He told me, and these are his exact words, 'If you don't get your shit together, you are going to commit suicide.'"

My insides churned as I tried my best to retain a neutral facial expression. I could not imagine a doctor voicing these thoughts to a patient, especially without providing an immediate referral for psychological treatment. And why wasn't he offering more surgery to correct obvious defects that were treatable? I had my complaints about aftercare in the eighties and early nineties, but I had never met someone so neglected, left without basic medical follow-up. The company she worked for had the resources and were very willing to do everything they could to support her. She should not have fallen through the cracks in this mysterious fashion.

"And he didn't offer any kind of plan to mitigate the obvious reason for your depression?"

"No. I'm so confused. I feel like my face is too overwhelming for them or something. Like no one is listening or able to do anything. My father has been my biggest advocate, but he can't always be with me at the appointments. He is busy with his own job and can't take a lot of time off," she said. "The docs wanted to cut off my fingers on both hands early on from fear of infection. I didn't know it at the time, but my dad asked if they were infected at that moment. When the doctor said no, my dad insisted they leave them alone. I'm so glad he was there. They don't look great or function very well, but at least I have my fingers. I'm not sure how you can help me, but it's really great to be able to talk to someone about all of this."

After several hours of intense sharing, we were both exhausted and made plans to meet again the next day.

I went back to my room, let myself in, and sat down on the bed. A wave of grief overtook me. I cried and cried, the tissue box next to me emptying slowly but surely, a pile of soiled puffs scattered on the coverlet.

As I pondered this woman's plight, the details of her story brought up so many questions. And emotions. For her and for me. I was so grateful for the follow-up care I had received at Irvine. First and foremost, that thought kept going round and round in my head. What would I have done in her place? I couldn't imagine how she was facing the public every day with the scars she wore for the world to see. She couldn't even properly smile to help someone get past the initial shock of seeing her red and contorted lip line.

She had resources, an insurance company willing to do whatever it took for her to improve her looks and physical function. It didn't make sense that nothing had been done for over two years to help her when she was all but begging the medical professionals in charge to make some improvements. If her burn center was this unwilling to step in and do something, maybe bringing her out to California would help? I could at least try to make that happen.

I ordered room service and waited for my salad to arrive. And a glass of red wine. I thought about her hands and the story of her father intervening for them. Had I given up too easily on my own fingers? Would my father, had he been there, have been able to stop them from amputating them all? A wrenching thought. The tears began again. I called the front desk for a piece of chocolate caramel pie to be added to my salad order. It was going to be a long night of pondering and grieving.

The next day I invited her to California to consult with my surgeon Dr. Furnas and a well-known Orange County psychiatrist. She needed a second opinion on many fronts. If her hospital wasn't willing to help her, the only recourse was to find another that would. I knew the value of a plan and having reliable professionals a person could count on.

I couldn't do the inner work required for her to reinvent herself, to find a new normal. But lining up a course of action was one thing I could do to make a difference. I knew many existed just like her, men and women trying to find resources and practical help. Many wanted to get off a permanent disability path and mindset and try to carve out a place of meaning for themselves. And it made me more committed than ever to help aftercare become a priority in every burn center.

* * *

A few months after the training in Michigan, I flew to New Orleans for a similar venture at Children's Hospital of New Orleans. This not-for-profit pediatric medical center had a plastic and reconstructive surgery department that provided care for burn patients and kids with facial anomalies.

The provided hotel room and its location were perfect for someone who had never experienced this great Southern city. On a whim, I called Amy to see if she could join me. It would be a good opportunity for hands-on practice and follow-up to the training we did at her center. Cloaking it in those terms convinced her supervisor to send her down my way.

We worked hard, training a new group of staff about image enhancement and the behavioral skills. We tallied up one more department that had the tools and understanding to really help their patients post-discharge regarding aftercare needs.

If we had an added benefit of eating and sipping our way through the French Quarter, lucky us. We were both such foodies, especially enjoying the hot spicy Cajun and Creole temptations. From jalapeno to habanero, we could handle the dishes designed to disintegrate one's insides. My hands fared more poorly than my stomach, however. For one lunch, the Original French Market Restaurant and Bar, noted for its seafood and ice-cold drinks, drew us for their boiled crawfish platter. After diving in to peel the mound of spicy crawfish, my little hand began to fiercely burn. I had to run to the bathroom and rinse it under cold water to soothe the irritated skin. I then asked for ice from the waiter to try and cool it down. The taste was worth all the drama and kept us laughing for the rest of the day.

For our last evening, I made reservations at three different restaurants to maximize our palate-enhancement experience. We started with appetizers at one restaurant, followed by the main course at Emeril's, an extremely tough place for which to get a reservation. A social worker at Children's had a fortunate connection to secure two seats for the evening, and we had dessert at the fourth stop of the night.

A bit of work and a bit of tomfoolery. Some days it was nice to not take ourselves too seriously. The dream we found ourselves sharing had the lofty goal of seeing every burn center in the country with an aftercare program that could impact their patients' community reentry. We had new inroads to discover, but they needed to be tempered with self-care to keep the weight of the recovery world off our shoulders.

Amy and I couldn't do this alone.

13

The Umbrella

On a Sunday afternoon in the spring of 1998, I was chatting with Amy on the phone, sitting at my desk with my feet propped up on my home office desk, a mug of steaming coffee in front of me.

"Barbara, I have a question for you. What do you think about me applying to be the executive director of the Phoenix Society?"

My feet dropped to the floor. Silence ensued from my end for many long seconds.

"Amy, why in the hell would you want to do that? You have a fabulous secure job as the nurse manager at a renowned burn center where you've really made an impact with aftercare programs. You would be risking everything because the Phoenix Society is not respected in all circles of burn care."

"I realize the risk, but I think I can help the organization expand its vision of peer support for those living with a burn injury by working closer with the burn centers. The work will have national reach. All the things we talk about with aftercare and community reintegration…Phoenix could take the lead. We could build it into something great."

While I was still reeling from the idea, she rattled off a list of plans, her words flowing and her voice enthused.

"Barbara, will you write a letter of recommendation to the Board of Directors for me? You've been on the Board, and they have a lot of respect for you. Your backing could be important."

While I loved the organization, I also knew its reputation had suffered during recent years. Bridging the gap between a grass-roots fly-by-the-seat-of-your-pants structure to an organization that garners the respect of medical professionals would be a colossal challenge.

"Amy, I'm not sure this is the right move, but I will write that letter. As a survivor, you have insights about recovery. As a nurse, you understand the medical world. Maybe with your drive and commitment, you can bridge the chasm."

When I sat down to write the letter of recommendation, the words and key points came so effortlessly, it felt divinely inspired. My letter outlined all the ways I believed her to be especially qualified for the position. She was the nurse manager of a burn center, a survivor herself, an active member of the American Burn Association, and an aftercare advocate who had begun many support programs already. I still recall the last sentence of the letter: *I recommend hiring Amy Acton because she is pure gold.*

In the fall of 1998, the Phoenix Society Board hired Amy to be the director. She started her job using a tiny office at Blodgett Medical Center in Grand Rapids, Michigan, with one year's salary in the organization's coffer. If she couldn't raise enough money for the second year, it would all be a wash, and the organization dissolved.

Amy clarified the mission of the Phoenix Society early on in her tenure: "To provide support through education, collaboration, advocacy, and peer support to those touched by a burn injury." Put in layman's terms, "No survivor should have to do it alone."

We talked on the phone often.

"Barbara, peer support needs to be one of our first goals. I want to form a national committee to begin brainstorming, and I need you on it."

I had to give her credit for incredible vision, warranted or not at this point, yet to be proven. But recognizing her fearless leadership, I jumped in with both feet.

And my heart.

"You know I'm with you, Amy. Just tell me when and where."

She assembled a committee of nine members to organize and develop materials for the peer support national standardized program. I had a place at the table, along with a select group of burn care professionals and survivors. Among them were a social worker, a chaplain, two burn nurses who were survivors, a communications professor, a nonprofit associate, and a psychiatric nurse.

We gathered near my home in Sedona, Arizona, for one of our first meetings. Ken had fallen in love with Sedona on our visit as tourists in 1990, shortly after our marriage. It had been voted one of the best places to retire, and Ken agreed with the sentiment. After a few years of cajoling, he persuaded me to give it a try. We bought a house we both loved and have enjoyed the mild climate, artsy community, and beautiful red rock buttes surrounding the city ever since.

The local fire chief offered our group his main conference room. The stucco brick station had a picture-perfect setting, tucked back from Highway 89A in West Sedona with magnificent views from every window. We spent our first day talking about the positive and negative aspects of a peer support program.

One of the burn nurses began the dialogue. "My administrator will definitely need convincing this program is a good idea. We have had a lot of negative experiences—survivors coming in and giving out erroneous information, offering medical and legal advice, or trying to sell the perfect itch-free skin care line. We need to be very careful how we screen and train people."

"I think we all can agree that a peer support initiative must meet strict criteria for a burn center to buy into it," Amy said. "We must be very intentional to develop a medical model–based program that can be reproduced with checks and balances to maintain it."

"I imagine the program in every single burn center in the country. That should be our goal," I said.

"Do you think that's realistic?" one of the nurses asked.

"Why not?" I asked back.

"Let's just take this one step at a time," Amy said. "How about we start by brainstorming what areas we need to cover in the training…"

We spent two days making lists and hashing out the nuances of what we deemed absolutely essential for the training. The first binder we put together consisted of twenty pages of materials, a fraction of what it would be a decade later at 150, including instructor and coordinator training materials. Coming up with a name was one of the toughest tasks we faced. The group bounced around ideas.

"Peer Support Network."

"Healing Through Peer Support."

I was half listening, focusing on what peer support meant to me as I thought about possible names. I kept starting with the word *survivor*.

*Survivors helping others…Survivors offering help…Survivors assisting others…*And then I blurted out, "I've got it! SOAR. Survivors Offering Assistance in Recovery."

Some of the committee members thought the name fit well. A few disagreed. We decided to sit on it for a while and see if something better popped up. I liked the concept of soaring and what it implied for one survivor to help another sprout wings to get back to life.

The name was eventually adopted, and the Phoenix SOAR program was launched.

While teaching the social skills had always been my first priority in the programs I developed, I understood the value of offering peer support for patients early in their recovery. In my mind, we were killing two birds with one stone as peer supporters could be taught the tools and use them in their interactions with new survivors. They would be able to impart them with experiential knowledge behind the words, offering a credible example because they have lived it.

These reentry tools could have a profound effect on a survivor's relationship to the public. The world wasn't going to change. We lived in a society generally committed to first impressions that often created false judgments. We had to adapt. Society equated disfigurement with imperfection, often resulting in responses of fear, rejection, and social discomfort. Establishing programs to assist survivors with social skills and image enhancement was vital in the adaptation process.

SOAR was officially launched the third year of Amy's directorship. We piloted the SOAR project in six burn centers, all of them having a prior link with the Phoenix Society. We started by training the coordinators and a small room of burn survivors associated with the pilot hospitals at the World Burn Congress in Grand Rapids. One of the key benefits to a burn center is that the program enables them to create a pool of motivated and trained peer supporters with a minimum expenditure of staff resources.

One of the things we learned in our first training is that new coordinators need time to gather a team of qualified peer supporters. We began to return and conduct the day-long peer support class at Phoenix World Burn Congress in Grand Rapids, once the coordinators were on board and fully understood their role and the role of the peer supporter. Part of the day involved vetting the survivors to make sure they were far enough along on the recovery path to truly support someone else. We monitored the programs for half a year in each center, making changes as needed. After seeing the successes, we made plans to expand into more centers as we were invited.

I began to help with the hospital-based training on a regular basis. As additional centers took on the program, the potential grew. Having gained confidence in where the Phoenix Society was heading, I decided to work more intentionally to promote the organization. I made them the umbrella for my programs. We meshed well.

In the early years of Amy's leadership, we were, at times, discouraged by the slow progress being made reaching one burn center at a time. But then we would look at the survivors with cleft palates and those with other facial anomalies. They had no umbrella organization to unite under, with only small pockets of support here and there. We wanted our umbrella to expand. Every individual with a facial or body difference and their families could benefit from the support and tools offered by the Phoenix Society.

The umbrella theme took on more ideas as we moved forward. Amy and I met up in Chicago at the annual 2003American Burn Association meeting. This conference brought together over a thousand burn care professionals from all over the country as well as other nations. Much of the focus centered on new research and ideas for the medical side of the burn equation.

I had been one of the few survivors attending these conferences since the early eighties, helping with a breakout session or two on post-hospitalization issues and aftercare. Amy had been involved since the late eighties, but now in her new role, she would be representing the Phoenix Society.

We set up the Phoenix Society booth in the main hall of the Convention Center. Promoting SOAR was high on our list of goals for the week. At this point, we had twenty hospitals on board with our program. That left multiple burn centers yet on our radar. I had just attended one of the psych-social breakout sessions and needed to vent.

"Amy, you know I love the ABA, but every year I listen to the same papers being given by different people—okay, sometimes the same people—worked fifty different ways…cataloguing how *challenged* we survivors are and *dysfunctional* and blah, blah, blah… They keep logging the problems but never give any solutions. What's the point?"

"I hear your frustration, Barbara. We are passionate about the solutions and want them to be the focus, but they're just not there yet. When I was working on the unit as a nurse, I didn't know what to do either. I straddled both worlds as a survivor and medical care professional, but they didn't intermingle at first. We have to balance our passion with reality. We have to help them understand there are tools available…"

"I know, I know…You have more patience than I do. I'm going to turn into a screaming shrew one of these years. I'm just warning you…"

Amy smiled and shook her head. She usually had a way of talking me off the ledge. One of the things I have always valued about our friendship is her steady, cool head in the midst of conflict and what looked like dead-end endeavors.

"No, you won't. I know this stuff is close to your heart, Barbara. What we do really well, I think, is to bring people together. The Phoenix Society is a vehicle. We just need an awakening, and I think it'll happen slowly but surely. People who want to give back don't have to do it on their own. They can plug into a whole community and structure that already exists and help propel it forward. That will be the key to real inroads being made."

"Amy, you certainly have the vision. Building partnerships. Not reinventing the wheel. You were on the right track when you decided to take this risk. Truthfully. From that first phone call. Okay, I promise to be patient, which is not a strength of mine, and trust that we are going to make progress," I said.

We began to build a team at the Phoenix Society of staff and volunteers who were committed to the long-term and psychosocial needs of survivors and their families. Pam Peterson, a former burn nurse, joined the team, and she helped to expand the SOAR program and the Phoenix World Burn Congress. Amy Clark, a child life specialist, worked part-time building family programs and content, such as the Journey Back, our school reentry program. We began a newsletter, *Burn Support News,* and distributed it to many burn centers, survivors, and foundations.

One of the early adopters of the SOAR program was Regions Burn Center in Saint Paul, Minnesota. Dr. Solem was a strong advocate of the work we were doing. As part of his presidential year at the ABA, he asked the Phoenix Society to arrange for a general session to be presented by a panel of burn survivors, sharing their successes and struggles during recovery. We brought awareness to the burn care providers regarding the long-term challenges of community reentry. We shared the available tools to ease this gap in care.

The next big break came when the Phoenix Society was asked to present the burn survivor's perspective on the priorities of research over the next ten years at the Burn State of the Science meetings in 2006. Amy Acton, Chris Gilyard, and Erin Mounsy presented, and I participated in the discussion groups. Although we were the last session on the last day, both Chris and Erin shared their personal experience of spiraling after discharge into dark places because of the lack of aftercare and support for reentry.

Our presentation had the intended impact to help the burn team professionals hear *the hard truth softly.* Dr. Greenhalgh, the president of the American Burn Association at this time, stood up after the panel discussion and stated the need for a joint committee between the ABA and the Phoenix Society to work more closely together to address the long-term needs of the survivor community. The joint Aftercare and Reintegration Committee was established that year. Dr. Greenhalgh and Amy presented together at the presidential general session, and the number of burn centers engaging with the Phoenix Society soared.

Finally, there was a number to call for survivors, mothers, teachers, therapists, and friends struggling with a post-hospitalization problem and needing help. Medical professionals often got bombarded with difficult issues they didn't know how to tackle down the road. The Phoenix Society wanted to be a greater source of information for them as well.

For the world.

I broached this very subject on my next phone call with Amy.

"I know you are the visionary, but I have an idea I need to run past you. You got a minute?"

"Yes. Go for it."

"I've been wondering about the future of my programs—Image Enhancement and BEST. Phoenix has been using them for years, but I think it's time to completely hand them over. What do you think of the idea of putting them online? So whether a survivor is in Sydney or Singapore or Seattle, they can easily access all of the tools?"

"Wow. I think that would be amazing. They could reach an endless number of people...We would have to raise some funds to make it happen, but I love the concept. Let's see what we can do."

In such a short time, I could hardly believe how integral the Phoenix Society had become in my concept of aftercare and creating an umbrella for survivors to flourish under. It was still a dream to have every burn center using the tools and programs as a standard of care.

I had hope that the chasm truly could be breached.

Truly building a community for transformational healing... bringing people together.

14

Awakenings

I exited the plane at Baltimore/Washington International Thurgood Marshall Airport on a sunny October afternoon. The 2005 Phoenix Society's World Burn Congress began the next day, with two local Baltimore hospitals, along with area firefighters, hosting the event.

I filed through the crowd on my way to baggage claim, looking for conference signs. As I glided down the escalator, a sea of firefighters in crisp blue uniforms could be seen below, waiting to help the attendees find the transport vans to City Center.

One of the group approached and introduced himself. His peppered gray hair and military-like stance shouted *seasoned fireman.*

"Hi! I'm Mark. Welcome to Baltimore. Let me help you with your bags."

"Barbara. And it's nice to meet you. Thanks."

We stood silently as we waited for my real luggage, two rather large suitcases filled with a ton of paraphernalia I would need for the crazy week ahead of me. He hefted them off the conveyor with little effort, and we headed for the exit doors.

"Mark, will you get a chance to attend any of the sessions?"

"A few. I have been assigned to run interference for the fire chief, so I will be around."

"Great. Thanks for your help," I said, stepping into the line for the next available vehicle.

The firefighters and hospital staff played key roles in hosting a World Burn Congress. It was Amy's idea to get them involved. It took people power in the form of a multitude of volunteers to help the eight hundred attendees check in for the four-day event.

The woman I sat next to in the van turned out to be a nurse at one of the Shriners Hospitals for Children from a neighboring state. This being her first conference, Diane confessed to being a little nervous about what to expect.

"I'm not quite sure why I'm here," she said. "I know this is a conference for survivors. My supervisor insisted I attend. How could I refuse?"

"Don't worry, Diane," I said. "Just attend the sessions and soak it in. We all take home something from each conference. I'm sure you'll see another perspective about burn care. And it's an opportunity to view the burn injury from the survivor and family perspective."

"Good point," she said with a smile that slowly faded, turning into a thoughtful frown. "But I get the feeling there's a bigger reason I've been sent here..."

Arriving at the hotel, we parted ways, and I headed to the check-in counter. My workshop started bright and early the next morning, and I had much to organize.

The next afternoon, I stood at the podium in one of breakout session rooms, pausing to look at the fifty or so faces in front of me before introducing myself. I was always thankful to see a good-sized group wanting to learn the tools for the Behavioral Enhancement Skills Training workshop. Usually there was a mix of survivors, family, and burn care practitioners in the audience. Today seemed no different. I saw a few pressure garment–clad attendees. It made me happy to have some "newbies" learning the reentry skills early in their recoveries.

I told a bit of my story and launched into the psychological aspects of dealing with a burn injury. The effects spread beyond the person lying in the hospital bed. For one exercise, we called up a mock family and discussed the issues each one faces when a family member is burned.

"So when Dad is in the hospital, what does Mom have to deal with?" I asked.

The audience called out ideas.

"Fighting fear that her husband will die."

"Fretting over each painful procedure administered to her man."

"Worrying if the kids are being taken care of."

"Having to communicate with extended family and friends."

"Wondering if she will lose her job and who will pay the bills."

"Stressing over the future and feeling like she has to be strong for everyone."

As the answers were given, I handed balloons to Mom, one for each issue. Soon she was unable to hold on to all of them, and some fell to the floor. It was a vivid picture of the stress and myriad of challenges someone in her place experiences. Keeping all the balloons in the air is a daunting task after a family member is burned.

"Good list," I said. "Okay, how about the teenage son?"

We went through each family member, focusing on the unique pressures and problems each person could face. A big portion of the workshop gave the attendees the opportunity to learn and practice the tools. I taught the importance of STEPS, Rehearse Your Responses (RYR), and the Staring Tool.

We began with STEPS (Self-Talk, Tone of Voice, Eye Contact, Posture, and Smile) and practiced how it felt not to use them and to use them. The attendees quickly realized intuitively the power of STEPS in their lives. Each saw that they had personal responsibility for and control over how others responded to their burns.

To learn RYR, everyone wrote a three-sentence answer to a question asked about their burn, and then the group formed two circles facing each other. We spent the next twenty minutes taking turns, both asking questions and sharing responses. The staring tool was followed by learning concrete ways to handle the fake gawks, double takes, and strange looks mimicked for practice. Everyone participated, and the crowd got in a few laughs from blunders and awkward moments. But no one left without new practical knowledge.

At the end of the four-hour session, a thirty-something guy approached me. "Barbara, thank you for this workshop. My name is Dan, and I've been a physical therapist at my burn center for ten years. So many times I have discharged patients and worried about them going to grocery stores and walking around out there with their masks and scars. I didn't know how to prepare them. I never knew about the tools," he said.

"Dan, I'm so glad you found this workshop and feel like it will be helpful. Yes, spread the word, and train other staff at your center," I pleaded.

"I will. I finally have something concrete to share, and I can't wait to get back and help in a whole new way."

As I gathered up my teaching props and notes, straightening the room before I left, I felt gratitude for the privilege of sharing the tools that spurred me on to go anywhere and try anything. They helped me thrive. As I headed back to my hotel room, my mind focused on the next phase of the conference for me—the image-enhancement makeup consultations.

The next morning, I was doing the final setup for the makeovers. With a one-hour slot for each survivor, we tried to maximize the opportunity to include the application and teaching time. If a survivor couldn't replicate the simple daytime makeup back home, then we had failed. This wasn't anything like your typical department store makeover. We were not going for glamour or flamboyance. We wanted to create a basic, everyday natural look that helped the person feel comfortable out and about in daily life.

We divided the room for the makeovers into eight stations with an array of brushes, creams, foundation and blush colors, lipsticks, and eye shadows at each one. The Society of Plastic and Surgical Skincare Specialists provided their elite medical model expertise. Each esthetician worked in a medical setting with a board-certified plastic surgeon. Scars and skin discoloration did not faze them. Their acceptance and warmth created a safety and trust that was palpable in the room. Magic happened as the survivors witnessed their faces transformed.

Sometimes a family member would come in with their loved one, then hover in protective mode. Unless a survivor seemed extremely fragile, we asked the family member to wait in a chair on one side of the room and be surprised by the transformation.

A gentleman named Emmitt was our only male candidate for the morning session. He was a tall muscular African-American man dressed in jeans and a sports shirt. He had visible scars on his cheeks and forehead and some discoloration along his neck and jawline. I escorted him to his station and probed a bit about his life.

"What kind of work do you do, Emmitt?" I asked.

"I used to be in direct sales, but I lost that job after the fire. My boss reassigned me to working the phone lines, believing the company would lose profits if customers saw my scars. But I hate cold calls—I do so much better if I can look a customer in the eye."

"Well, let's see what we can do for you. Jeannine will be your esthetician. I will check back on your progress in a bit," I said.

My role took me from station to station, observing, supervising, giving my opinion if needed, and helping everything run smoothly. We took before and after pictures, wanting each survivor to see the transformation.

When I checked back on Emmitt and Jeannine, he was picking up the mirror to see the final result. I watched as his eyes registered shock. Silent tears formed, then fell down his cheeks. His big shoulders began to shake. I put my hand on his arm, letting him absorb the moment. It took a bit for him to find his voice.

"I think...with this...I can get my old job back." A wide grin slowly formed amid the tears. A satisfied nod bobbed in the mirror.

I squeezed his shoulder in support. "I think you're right, Emmitt. Your boss made a hasty call that he probably didn't need to. But it all starts with you. The makeup's just a tool. If you believe you can do it, people will take their cues from you."

During lunch, I ran to the main hall to grab a bite to eat and, hopefully, have a few minutes to listen in on the open microphone session directly following. Survivors were given a chance to pick up a microphone and tell what brought them to the World Burn Congress. The stories poured out, sometimes hesitantly, often grueling. Words of loss, pain, courage, and hope.

A young woman in the far back started the litany.

"Hi, I'm Karen." She paused and took a deep breath. "I'm…I'm thankful to be here. I guess I can't really sugarcoat my story…You see, my father abused me growing up."

Her head bowed down for a few seconds and then lifted, her eyes trying to find a spot to rest upon.

"When I became a teenager and started dating, he flipped out. He put a bomb in my car that left me with severe burns to my legs."

Another long pause. And then a whisper.

"He wanted me to die…"

Her voice got stronger.

"But here I am. He's in jail. I'm trying to forgive him…I wasn't sure I wanted to come to this conference. I'm glad I did—but…it's hard…"

She held out the mic, reaching for a friend to clutch through her tears.

The next survivor to share stood up, a man with half-formed tattoos amid scar patterns on his arms and neck. His voice was deep and a bit gruff.

"My name is Reggie, and I was burned four years ago this December. I was trying to start an old car and poured some gas down the carburetor—stupid, I know. It caused an explosion. But the worst thing is that my ten-year-old son was nearby and got burned with me…"

He paused and cleared his throat to stop the tears.

"And the guilt is hard to deal with, you know? I don't care about my scars, but he has his whole life in front of him…I wish I could take back those moments, but I can't. Thanks for listening."

The last person to share for the session was a young man with obvious burns on his hands, arms, and the side of his face.

"When I was a teenager, I was camping with some friends, and one of the guys threw some gas on our campfire to get it going. The exploding flame hit my shirt and caught it on fire. The guys tackled

157

me and ripped my shirt off, but the damage was done. Going to burn camp for several years really helped my recovery and taught me I'm not alone. Then I was fortunate enough to be awarded a Phoenix Education Grant [PEG] scholarship to go to college. I'm married now, and I have two young kids. I feel pretty lucky to be standing here at Phoenix World Burn Congress and meeting so many great people."

The open microphone sessions could be overwhelming, but played a vital role. It was often a survivor's first step in fully acknowledging the injury and asking for support.

A huge step toward recovery.

The applause and hugs from the audience affirmed life.

* * *

That evening, a large group of us headed over to the National Aquarium in Baltimore's inner harbor for a social outing together. The nonprofit public aquarium boasted seventeen thousand specimens of aquatic life. We wound around the structure from display to display, some of us wheelchair bound, others practically bouncing from the dolphins to the stingrays, oohing and aahing over the beautiful and fascinating sea life.

Pausing at a large tank of jellyfish, a teenager named Carrie asked to speak to me. Used to spontaneous conversations like this one, I readily agreed. We grabbed a bench together along the wall.

"Barbara, I need some advice, and I think you might have some insight. I'm graduating from high school in the spring and will be heading off to college next fall. My burn injury occurred when I was three—something to do with scalding water. I have very few memories of it all, but living with the scars has impacted me a lot. But the thing is…my mom will never talk about it. I feel like I need to put the pieces together, but I'm afraid to push her for answers because I don't want to upset her. What can I do? I want to be sensitive, but this is my life, and I'm mad that she doesn't get it."

"Carrie, sadly, your story is very common. I think parents feel a lot of guilt if the injury is perceived as somehow their fault. Their whole focus is helping you, and they don't realize they could use some processing with a professional themselves. Instead, the shame and guilt get shoved deep, and it becomes too painful to talk about over the years. Unintentionally, your mom may have made herself a victim and kept you in that mode too."

"So we are talking about years of stuff I can't fix. What can I do? I don't want to be a victim. I'm a survivor."

"I know you are afraid to upset her, but you can share bits of your journey with her, things you're realizing. You seem so well adjusted. You have plans for your life. Focus on those positives, and be an example of someone in touch with her feelings. It may take some time, but look for ways to express both your victories and your needs as you put this puzzle together. I think if you frame it as you needing to make sense of some things, your mom will want to help. And in helping you, she may make some discoveries for herself."

"All right. I will try. Thanks for listening. Sorry for dumping all of that on you. I'm so glad there are people I can talk to about this."

She gave me a hug and walked off to catch up with her group.

I pondered her situation, hoping my advice would have some effect down the road.

The next two days flew by in similar fashion. Running from session to session, I found joy in interacting with new friends and old. What the conference did best was to bring people together. The Phoenix Society existed as a support system for everyone, both survivors and family members. There was power in sharing our stories and journeying together. A sense of empowerment increased with each speaker, workshop, and new friendship.

People with hidden burns, who had lived for years only wearing long-sleeved shirts, put on a tank top. People who had gone for decades having never met any other survivors found a group of friends who understood them at a deep level. People who had lost loved ones in a fire came and found a new sort of family. The conference became a place to receive encouragement, to go back to one's community and live more fully.

By the last day of the conference, I was ready to celebrate at the closing dinner. With all the sessions finished and my gear packed up for an early morning flight out, I paused to reflect on the week. Everyone dressed a little fancy, and we began the night with appetizers and drinks. I shared a table with some dear friends and Ken, who had joined me several days into the conference.

Getting out on the dance floor after dinner finished the night off perfectly. It was good to see survivors and their loved ones enjoying themselves. On my way back to my table after a dance, I ran into Diane, the nurse who sat next to me in the van the first day.

"Barbara, you were right," she said.

Trying to remember our conversation, I asked the obvious. "How was I right?"

"There is a reason I came to this conference! I have gained so much insight. I always tell my patients that their grafts look good and they are healing well to mixed reactions. I never really thought about it, but now I understand that when I am praising the grafts, the reality they are thinking about is 'Yesterday my skin was perfect, and today it is scarred and will never look the same again.' And I'm more aware of the struggles after discharge and returning to the community."

She paused, shaking her head.

"Now I see how insensitive I was by assuming my words were helping them. I'm going to be a better nurse after this conference. I finally get it—or at least more than I did before."

I loved seeing burn center staff looking beyond the care in the burn center to the vital role they have the opportunity to play in the community reentry process. Phoenix World Burn Congress touches many people in a multitude of ways.

The thought became reinforced early the next day as we waited in line to take a bus back to the airport. The firemen showed up at our hotel in the cool of the morning just before dawn, loading and unloading. I recognized the fireman grabbing my bag from our encounter five days ago.

"Mark. What did you think of the conference?" I asked.

He stopped and faced me.

"Truthfully?" he asked, lowering his eyes and then raising them again to meet mine. "I used to think survivors hated me for saving their lives. Now I see how wrong I was to think that. It's freeing…and it makes me want to be more involved with such a brave community."

Powerful words coming from a fireman.

I gave him a hug, whispering my thanks.

15

An Intertwining

I define home as family, belonging, appreciation, and comfort. Though I have lived in many places, I have had few homes. My Iowa farmhouse as a child was one, more so before my father died. Ken and I have created a loving and joyful life together. But there is another place that has come to be like home in a surprising way.

The UCI Medical Center has been a part of my existence since that fateful day in 1977. The hospital has transitioned from a county hospital with a burn unit open-ward configuration to a modern medical facility with a state-of-the-art burn center. My relationship has ebbed and flowed over the years. I have been a burn and rehab patient, volunteer burn support group leader, and board member for two philanthropic organizations: UCI Associates and the Orange County Burn Association. I also coordinated an Image Enhancement Center for the Chao Comprehensive Cancer Center for a decade. In this ever-growing and changing mega-institution, UCI has always tugged at my heart. And I am always interested in the next great advancement, particularly with the burn center.

An intertwining.

Walking with others through pain fosters connections like nothing else. I have been involved in the burn survivor community for thirty-five years and still ponder what full retirement looks like for me. I'm not ready to give up on my dream of making more inroads, creating a bigger umbrella, and getting every single burn center in the country on board with community reintegration. But there are also moments to stop, reflect, and celebrate the journey.

In the fall of 2013, I received a phone call from Ruth Lott, a fellow board member of the UCI Associates, asking me to be the keynote speaker for a special UCI event honoring critical care nurses in Southern California. Having always admired the nursing profession and honored to be asked, I willingly agreed. I have long believed that my own nurses helped turn the tide for my recovery during many dark days. Their role went beyond the practical to the heartfelt, reaching the spirit of a patient. I still recall Clara bringing in a small toothbrush from her home for me, one that would fit a mouth tightened by scar tissue. I think of a first-year nurse, Beth, calmly explaining each procedure, distracting me with stories about her love life and sports to help me endure.

Honoring their profession felt right.

Because it was from the heart and a love note to nurses, my presentation came together easily. The event was held at an upscale restaurant in Irvine, Andrei's Conscious Cuisine, with over two hundred people in attendance. The majority of the group consisted of elite trauma and wound nurses from three surrounding counties. I also invited some people close to my heart: my dearest lifelong friend Judy, my stepdaughter Jennifer and granddaughter Heather, my beloved Dr. David Furnas and his wife Mary Lou, several of my former junior high students with families of their own, and a few key staff members from UCI. Given a special invitation were my two favorite nurses, Clara Rodriguez and Beth Lukina.

After a lovely buffet dinner in the Great Room with a choice of beef short ribs, saffron chicken, and artichoke and goat cheese ravioli, Ruth Lott stood up to address the group.

"Welcome nurses, UCI staff, and friends to this special event. I have known Barbara Kammerer Quayle for many years, and though she keeps telling me she is retired, looking at her activities, I never really believed, hence the invitation tonight."

If I could have blushed, I would have at her praise. But my facial grafts didn't have the blood supply to turn pink on their own. Instead, I walked up to the front of the room and turned to face the group, avoiding the ominous podium. With my short height, no one would be able to see me, nor the tools I use whenever I share my story: STEPS, hand gestures, humor, and walking a bit through the audience.

The first words from my mouth surprised even me. I raised my arms above my head in a Rocky victory gesture and shouted, "I! Love! Nurses!"

The wild applause was a good start to the evening. I captured their undivided attention and fostered an immediate connection. This wasn't going to be their usual clinical, talking-head medical lecture. I clicked to my first slide: my school picture as a teacher taken right before my car crash. The blouse I wore with a long pointed collar and the bright blue eyeshadow usually drew a smile or two.

"Nearly three decades ago, my burn injury occurred…and with it, my life changed dramatically."

I shared a brief overview of the details and then put up a slide of my primary care nurse, Clara, and me.

"The title of my presentation tonight is 'The Five Gifts to Bestow Upon Your Patients: A Burn Survivor's Perspective.' The first gift both Clara and Beth gave me was treating me as a person, not a diagnosis. They took the time to ask questions about my life, gathering clues about me from personal items in my room and from people who visited. Asking questions about a patient's life conveys true interest and care."

I saw several heads in the audience nodding in agreement, thoughtful looks being sent my way. I went on to share about the gifts of empathy, a reassuring warm tone of voice, and attentively listening.

"As patients, we are in ultra-sensitive mode. Voices carry everything, concern or distance. I knew the residents who walked into my room who were invested in my care and those who were just putting in the time until their next rotation. We see and sense everything."

More affirmative nodding from the audience.

"The final gift is the gift of hope. Don't let fear stop you from envisioning a bright future for your patients. However, do not lie. And do not predict that someone will play tennis again or go back to the same job again, unless you are certain. Tell them about former patients who have lived with this kind of injury and lived well. That might take on the form of providing peer support to convey the message, helping your patient to actually meet a survivor who is further down the road of recovery. My occupational therapist had the vision to do that for me. Discuss community reentry before discharge, and talk about available support groups and organizations like the Phoenix Society to connect with. Don't assume they will find these resources on their own."

I gave the attendees a chance to ask questions after the main section of my presentation. They ran the gamut: How could they better motivate their patients? What is the most helpful thing a nurse ever said to me? How did I know who cared about me as a person and who didn't? What could they do to better be able to relate to their patients? Was this presentation available anywhere so they could share it with their units?

My final PowerPoint slides were personal, blessings and thanks I wanted to bestow on key people in the room. I clicked on a picture of Beth and me to begin the litany. A colleague was standing off to the side, ready to hand me bouquets of flowers to present to dear and lifelong friends.

"Beth, thank you for coming tonight. With Clara not being able to attend, you have stepped up to represent the two of you. You truly helped save my life, and the gifts you gave me encouraged me throughout my recovery. Please accept these flowers as a small gift to you."

As Beth stood up, I met her at the front of the room and handed her the bouquet. She accepted the flowers with a smile amid great applause and encircled me in a heartfelt hug. She returned to her chair around the head table, and I braced myself to continue.

Holding back tears, I clicked on the next slide, a photo of Dr. Furnas in his usual white coat and me standing together. I have tenaciously kept in touch with him over the years. A visit to Orange County rarely goes by without Ken and I meeting David and Mary Lou for lunch or dinner. He has been my cheerleader by supporting my aftercare endeavors through the decades, and I consider our relationship one of the most special of my life. Alongside the photo of us were his words about crisis, written for a Who's Who in America publication back in the eighties:

"Crisis: A *crisis*, at the onset, usually augers nothing but ill. In the long run, however, my *crises* have more often than not marked a new course in my life, which is more fulfilling, and more exciting than anything in the past. Yes, a bit of good luck is needed, but the special feature of a crisis is that you are suddenly cut off from past patterns, habits, and interdependencies. Along with the distress and pain is freedom! Freedom to build again, with a new foundation and modern structure, using wisdom you didn't have the last time you built."

Even though his words were about himself and the crises in his own life, I've always felt they certainly were applicable to burn survivors and our recoveries. A burn injury can mark a new course in one's life, which often is more fulfilling and more exciting than anything in the past. Yes, a bit of good luck is needed, and we can build again with a new foundation and modern structure, using wisdom we didn't have the last time we built. I've shared this with hundreds of burn survivors, professionals, and friends.

"Dr. Furnas, you gave me my life back with your surgical skills and encouragement. We truly had a partnership on the journey of my recovery. I can only say 'thank you,' but the words go so much deeper."

He seemed surprised and touched by the recognition, a retired surgeon ten years out of the hospital setting. He stood up and moved to the front, giving me his much-loved giant hug. I continued to fight the tears as he returned to his seat, the audience still applauding.

My next-to-the-last slide was a picture of Judy, standing with her arms raised amid a profusion of flowers around her, a glowing smile on her face.

"Judy, you have so generously given me the gift of love, loyalty, and support over so many years, through my recovery and far beyond. You are the sister I never had, and I love you dearly."

A stunned-to-the-extreme Judy wiped her own tears as she walked to the front of the room, shaking her head at me, but the look on her face showed how touched she was by the moment. I handed her a special bouquet of her favorite blooms. We clung to each other for a few seconds. We smiled.

She whispered, "Oh, Barbara. I'm so shocked. You know how I love you."

As she went back to her table, I clicked on my last slide. I had to end on a God-note. A beloved gentleman from my church spoke a few words long ago that had never left me. I needed to pass them on.

When a crisis happens, remember—you are not alone. God is in control, and something good will come of this.

I finished with a few words of my own. "Thank you for the gifts you will keep giving your patients. You. Matter."

The crowd began to clap. They rose to their feet. I stood mute, so aware of how far I had ventured on my personal and career path, overwhelmed by the feeling that it all truly had meaning—every choice to persevere, to stretch my wings, to risk, to chase my dreams.

All intertwined.

A sense of being home.

A FEW MORE THOUGHTS AND REFLECTIONS

———

These irregular and uneven shaped pearls are one-of-a-kind called Baroque pearls. No two pearl beads are alike in size and shape, and there in lies their beauty. They could be viewed as undesirable and unacceptable because they are not perfectly even and round. However, I find they are beautiful and *perfect in their imperfection* much like burn survivors and many people with a facial or body difference.

There is beauty in the pearls and the people when viewed in their uniqueness and

There's an expression I frequently use "TANA" (There Are No Accidents) which sums up my burn injury. In reflecting over the years, I have found this to be true. From those in the burn center through rehab, reconstructive surgeries, resuming teaching, beginning the School Reentry, Social Skills, and Image Enhancement programs, an abundance of people came to my side at the right time to heal, coach, support, and love me. God prepared me and moved me from a school classroom to a world classroom.

I had a lot of baggage to release and God prepared me for marriage to a wonderful and caring husband.

A Few Things I've Learned Along the Journey

If you act like a victim, people will treat you like a victim
Find a purpose in life that benefits others
Be grateful, very grateful
Make your bed
Be on time
When given a choice, be kind (even when it's hard)
Smile at others. It always sends a positive message
Not everyone is going to like me and I can't please everyone
Act "as if" until it becomes authentic
Stand up straight especially when you don't feel like it.

And to quote The Four Agreements by Don Miguel Ruiz:

1. Be impeccable with your word.
2. Don't take anything personally ... my biggest challenge
3. Don't make assumptions
4. Always do your best

All in all, I am honored and privileged to be a burn survivor. I am grateful for this magnificent journey.

MONA KRUEGER BIO

———

Mona Krueger has dual masters in Social Work and Pastoral Studies. She has worked with the burn community both stateside and abroad since her burn injury in 1982 by writing survivor stories, leading support groups and facilitating peer support. She is currently the Aftercare Support Coordinator at the Legacy Emanuel Oregon Burn Center in Portland, Oregon. This is her third book in print. Mona's memoir, Sage Was The Perfect Shadow can be found on Amazon. Mona blogs at monakrueger.com.

CPSIA information can be obtained
at www.ICGtesting.com
Printed in the USA
BVHW032026040821
613543BV00013B/68